# CITY
# OF
# ANGELS

*The Applause Musical Library*

# CITY OF ANGELS

**Book by Larry Gelbart**

**Music by Cy Coleman**

**Lyrics by David Zippel**

**Introduction by Larry Gelbart**

**APPLAUSE**
**THEATRE BOOK PUBLISHERS**
211 WEST 71 STREET • NEW YORK NY • 10023

All inquiries concerning publication rights, including book club, translation and anthology rights, should be addressed to Applause Theatre Book Publishers, 211 West 71st Street, New York, NY 10023.

All inquiries concerning stock, amateur, second-class touring and foreign language stage performing rights should be addressed to Tams-Witmark Music Library, Inc., 560 Lexington Avenue, New York, NY 10022.

Inquiries concerning all other rights should be addressed to Albert I. Da Silva, Da Silva and Da Silva, 502 Park Avenue, New York, NY 10022.

*All photographs courtesy of and copyright © 1989, 1990 by Martha Swope.*

*Drawings by Al Hirschfeld are Copyright © 1989 by Al Hirschfeld and reproduced by special arrangement with Hirschfeld's exclusive representative, The Margo Feiden Galleries Ltd., New York.*

*Design by Gary Denys.*

**Library of Congress Cataloging-in-Publication Data**
Coleman, Cy.
   [City of angels. Libretto]
   City of angels / book by Larry Gelbart ; music by Cy Coleman ; lyrics by David Zippel ; introduction by Larry Gelbart.
      p.   cm. — (Applause musical library)
   Libretto of musical.
   ISBN 1-55783-080-0 : $19.95 — ISBN 1-55783-081-9 (pbk.) : $9.95
   1. Musicals — Librettos. I. Gelbart, Larry. II. Zippel, David. III. Title. IV. Series.
   ML50.C688C6 1990  <Case>
   782.1'4'0268—dc20                                                    90–1207
                                                                           CIP
                                                                            MN

APPLAUSE THEATRE BOOK PUBLISHERS
211 West 71st Street
New York, New York 10023

First Applause Printing, 1990.

# CONTENTS

(*Clockwise from top left*) Rachel York, Rene Auberjonois, Randy Graff, Scott Waara, Dee Hoty, James Naughton and Gregg Edelman.

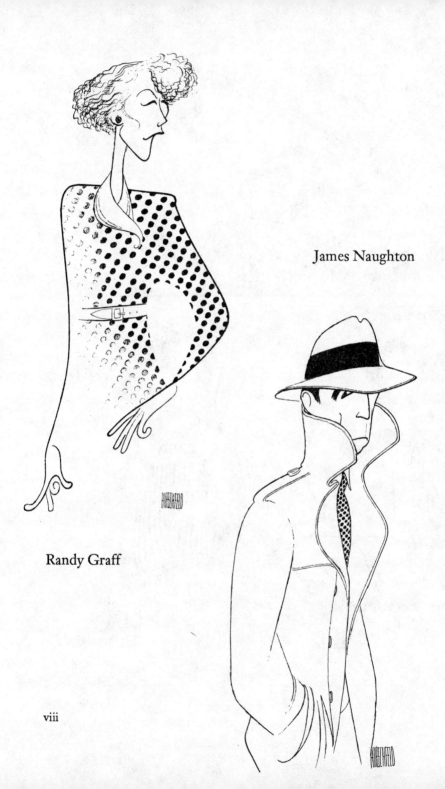

James Naughton

Randy Graff

# INTRODUCTION

In the late 1940's, I collaborated on a short-lived (four performances), long-forgotten revue for the Los Angeles stage called *My L.A.*

The dismal experience had two positive effects. The bug to write for the theater had been implanted so deeply it could only be removed by major surgery (such surgery usually performed by theater critics — and always without anesthesia). And it demonstrated for me, since all of the material dealt with life in Los Angeles, just how theatrically marvelous that marvelously theatrical city was, given the golden, orangey look of the Nathaniel West coast, the flamboyant flora, the exotic folk, each tinged by some degree of sunstroke; qualities that made the town that made the movies seem like a movie itself.

I just hoped that, somewhere down the freeway, I'd get another chance to use the city as the setting for a show, a show that would mercifully live for at least *five* performances.

Dissolve, as we members of the Writers Guild of America, West, are fond of saying, dissolve to December 11, 1989.

3

Exterior. Broadway. Night. Camera pans the black tie crowd arriving by stretch limos for the opening of a new musical comedy. The music is by Cy Coleman, the lyrics are by David Zippel and I've written the book. The show is called *City of Angels*, and it is set in the L.A. of the 40's. *My* L.A., the L.A. of those relatively innocent, post-war, pre-smog days. And not only have Cy, David and I dealt with the show-like aspect of the place, we've also written a movie that we've placed in the show.

For *City of Angels*, in telling the story of the novelist, Stine, offers the audience not only scenes from his life, but from his work, as well. His work being the adaptation of one of his books into a screenplay built around a fictional hero, an ex-cop named Stone, those scenes add up to an onstage mini-private eye movie — a shred of Chandler, a dash of Hammett, so to speak.

The result is a show that works on the twin levels of those hardy perennials, reality and fantasy. The *final* result, however, is a show that works on *four* levels. The third is achieved when Stine's character, Stone, steps out of the pages of the screenplay to confront Stine in the real world, to insist that his creator maintain the same moral values he ascribes to his fictional alter ego.

The fourth level, or the play-within-the-play-within-the-play-within-the-play, is created by having our actors play more than one role. For instance, in the screenplay portions of the show, Stone's secretary, Oolie, is played by the same actress who plays Stine's employer, the producer-director, Buddy Fidler's secretary, Donna.

In some instances, we first meet someone in the screenplay, say, Alaura Kingsley, and later discover the model for the character when the same actress appears as Buddy Fidler's wife, Carla Haywood.

We reverse the process by introducing Fidler himself, oozing fake charm, in Stine's life before revealing him in Stine's screenplay depicted as an equally odious studio boss, Irwin S. Irving, a man with absolutely no charm at all, real *or* fake.

It is our way of demonstrating how artists reward and/or punish the people in their private lives by the manner in which they portray them in their public works.

A case in point occurs in Act Two when Stine, accused of becoming a literary prostitute by his wife, Gabby, immediately bangs out a movie scene in which Stone discovers that the love of his life, Bobbi, has in fact become a literal prostitute. Both women, of course, are played by the same actress.

(It should be pointed out that Stine and Stone do not double. Each is played by a different actor.)

It is only when Stine, the writer, deals with his fictionalized version of those who populate his real life that he has any control over them. In reality, these role models are in no way guided by a few pecks at the keys of Stine's Corona. They have hearts and minds of their own. Stine may be able to think the same of the worldly Donna as he does of the simple minded Oolie, but Donna, he will come to learn to his great unhappiness, is very much Donna. She's not his creation, she's her own.

Lest any of this sound confusing, the reader is asked to remember that, when performed onstage, the show is color-coded: the real life passages staged in vivid colors, the reel life ones in glorious black and white — sets, costumes, props, everything but the actors' skin tones. Since we are never at a loss as to where we are, we are equally always sure of who is who.

This same sort of doubling took place during the creation of the show itself. Cy and David, though credited as composer and lyricist, also made an enormous contribution to the plotting and intricacy of the book. Ours was a bi-coastal collaboration since they're New Yorkers, while I live in Los Angeles, chiefly because I prefer to keep a firm grip on unreality.

After a year or so of collaborating via long distance calls, we decided that they were no substitute for some one-on-one, or, in our case, three-on-three meetings. Accordingly, Cy and David flew out to California, where we had a ten-day marathon session alongside one swimming pool or another in Beverly Hills and Palm Springs. That week and a half, we agreed, was the best work experience any of us had ever known. The sessions, in the parlance of jazz, really cooked.

Only one question nagged at me as we constructed our outline. At least half the time, *City of Angels* would be the enactment of Stine's screenplay. These scenes would be written to be staged as though they were straight out of a 1940's Sam Spade or Philip Marlowe film. Could the characters in these scenes *sing*? Could the integrity of the *film noir* Stine was writing be maintained if Stone, his private eye, and other cinematic characters suddenly burst into song?

The answer to the question turned out to be a very helpful second question:

How believable is it for *anyone* to sing in a musical

comedy? Especially in a reasonably modern American piece with none of the production trappings of another period?

By the time Cy and David returned to New York, we had come up with a scene-by-scene, song-by-song breakdown that proved, at least for us, so sound and durable that, with minor changes, it remained very much the same show that opened on Broadway.

With as complete a blueprint as we had devised, the actual writing took a comparatively short time to accomplish. I don't say that with any sense of smugness, certainly not with total satisfaction. For me, the best work is the work I hate to finish. When I'm involved with characters I like (on and off the page), work on a play is more play than work.

*City of Angels* was that kind of project. A lifelong movie fan, it was a treat for me to be able to write a 40's movie from the vantage point of the 80's, and, being able to write about the minefield a screenwriter has to run in Hollywood was, for me, one from the heart, one that's been dented from time to time by a few real life Buddy Fidlers, who live to fix what isn't broken, until it finally is.

Let me add quickly, for all three authors, that we most certainly exclude Michael Blakemore from the Buddy Fidler section of this world. As our director, Michael graced the entire project with a sense of objectivity and a generosity that enhanced all that he touched. While he contributed to every aspect of the production, from the book of the show to the look of the show, we never felt that one suggestion he made, not one of his rare demands was based on ego. Whatever glory he sought was for the show, not for himself. He put his hand to everything without leaving a single fingerprint.

Another of our heroes in this most collaborative of collaborations was Robin Wagner, whose sets, from the black and white mean streets of L.A. to the beige bedrooms of Bel-Air, were so totally in sync with our dramatic and musical vision of the show.

*City of Angels* was, for all of us, a labor of love. We invite you to join our affair.

Larry Gelbart
Beverly Hills
June 1990

# CITY OF ANGELS

# AWARDS

**New York Drama Critics Award** — Best Musical

**Tony Awards**
*Best Musical*
*Best Book of a Musical* — Larry Gelbart
*Best Original Score* — Cy Coleman (music), David Zippel
(lyrics)
*Best Leading Actor in a Musical* — James Naughton
*Best Featured Actress in a Musical* — Randy Graff
*Best Scene Design* — Robin Wagner

Nominated for Tony Awards were Michael Blakemore
(*Best Director*), Gregg Edelman (*Best Leading Actor in a
Musical*), Rene Auberjonois (*Best Featured Actor in a
Musical*), Florence Klotz (*Best Costume Design*), Paul Gallo
(*Best Lighting Design*)

**Drama Desk Awards**
*Outstanding Musical*
*Actor in a Musical* — James Naughton
*Featured Actress in a Musical* — Randy Graff
*Book of a Musical* — Larry Gelbart
*Music* — Cy Coleman
*Lyrics* — David Zippel
*Orchestrations* — Billy Byers
*Set Design* — Robin Wagner

**Outer Critics Circle Awards**
*Outstanding Broadway Musical*
*Outstanding Director* — Michael Blakemore
*Outstanding Design* — Robin Wagner (sets), Florence Klotz
(costumes), Paul Gallo (lighting)
*Special Award* — Larry Gelbart, for his contributions to
comedy

*City of Angels* was first presented by Nick Vanoff, Roger Berlind, Jujamcyn Theaters, Suntory International Corp., and The Shubert Organization at the Virginia Theatre, New York City, on December 11, 1989, with the following cast:

## MOVIE CAST
### (*In order of appearance*)

| | |
|---|---|
| STONE, *a private eye* | James Naughton |
| HOSPITAL ORDERLIES | James Hindman, Tom Galantich |
| OOLIE, *Stone's secretary* | Randy Graff |
| ALAURA KINGSLEY, *a femme fatale* | Dee Hoty |
| BIG SIX, *a thug* | Herschel Sparber |
| SONNY, *a smaller thug* | Raymond Xifo |
| JIMMY POWERS, *a movie crooner* | Scott Waara |
| THE ANGEL CITY 4 | Peter Davis, Amy Jane London, Gary Kahn, Jackie Presti |
| LT. MUNOZ, *a police detective* | Shawn Elliott |
| OFFICER PASCO, *a policeman* | Tom Galantich |
| BOBBI, *Stone's ex-fiancée* | Kay McClelland |
| IRWIN S. IRVING, *a movie mogul* | Rene Auberjonois |
| MAN IN PHONE BOOTH | James Hindman |
| PETER KINGSLEY, *Alaura's stepson* | Doug Tompos |
| MARGARET, *a maid* | Carolee Carmello |
| LUTHER KINGSLEY, *Alaura's husband* | Keith Perry |
| DR. SEBASTIAN MANDRIL | James Cahill |
| BUTLER | Evan Thompson |
| MALLORY KINGSLEY, *Alaura's stepdaughter* | Rachel York |
| MAN WITH CAMERA | Peter Davis |

| | |
|---|---|
| MAHONEY, *a studio press agent* | James Hindman |
| HARLAN YAMATO, *county coroner* | Alvin Lum |
| GAINES, *police commissioner* | Evan Thompson |
| GUARD | Tom Galantich |
| GIRL | Carolee Carmello |
| MARGIE, *a brothel keeper* | Eleanor Glockner |
| BOOTSIE, *a hooker* | Jacquey Maltby |

## HOLLYWOOD CAST
### (*In order of appearance*)

| | |
|---|---|
| STINE, *a writer of fiction* | Gregg Edelman |
| BUDDY FIDLER, *a movie director/producer* | Rene Auberjonois |
| SHOESHINE BOY, *a studio employee* | Evan Thompson |
| GABBY, *Stine's wife* | Kay McClelland |
| GILBERT, *Buddy's barber* | James Cahill |
| DONNA, *Buddy's secretary* | Randy Graff |
| ANNA, *Buddy's masseuse* | Eleanor Glockner |
| JIMMY POWERS | Scott Waara |
| THE ANGEL CITY 4 | Peter Davis, Amy Jane London, Gary Kahn, Jackie Presti |
| STUDIO ENGINEER | Evan Thompson |
| CARLA HAYWOOD, *Buddy's wife* | Dee Hoty |
| DEL DACOSTA, *a songwriter* | James Hindman |
| PANCHO VARGAS, *an actor* | Shawn Elliott |
| AVRIL RAINES, *a starlet* | Rachel York |
| GERALD PIERCE, *an actor* | Doug Tompos |

| | |
|---|---|
| WERNER KRIEGER, *an actor* | Keith Perry |
| STAND-IN | Carolee Carmello |
| CINEMATOGRAPHER | Alvin Lum |
| PROP MAN | Evan Thompson |
| GENE, *an assistant director* | Tom Galantich |
| BUDDY'S NEPHEW | James Hindman |
| SOUNDMAN | James Cahill |
| CLAPPERBOY | Peter Davis |
| STUDIO COPS | Herschel Sparber, Raymond Xifo |
| HAIRDRESSER | Eleanor Glockner |

*Swings*: Chrissy Faith, Marcus Neville

*Directed by* Michael Blakemore
*Musical Numbers Staged by* Walter Painter
*Scenic Design by* Robin Wagner
*Costumes Designed by* Florence Klotz
*Lighting Design by* Paul Gallo
*Sound Design by* Peter Fitzgerald *and* Bernard Fox
*Orchestrations by* Billy Byers
*Vocal Arrangements by* Cy Coleman *and* Yaron Gershovsky
*Musical Direction by* Gordon Lowry Harrell
*Fight Staging by* B.H. Barry
*Production Stage Manager*, Steven Zweigbaum
*General Manager*, Ralph Roseman

13

## ACT I

16

The place, Los Angeles; the time, the late 1940's.

# ACT I

*During the overture, the curtain rises to reveal a full-color movie poster, center:*

COMING SOON
CITY OF ANGELS
A BUDDY FIDLER PRODUCTION

*As the overture ends, three gunshots are heard. The movie poster fades to black and white. We hear an ambulance siren, hospital corridor sounds. The movie poster dissolves and flies.*

INT.     **A HOSPITAL CORRIDOR — NIGHT**

*The stage — semi-dark, bare, but for an overhead light above a hospital gurney, as it is wheeled downstage by* FIRST ORDERLY. *On it lies the still form of* STONE.

STONE'S VOICE (*Over*):   "No sense kicking about death. No point arguing with the ump. For my money, checking out in your sleep gets the nod, the big nod, every time. Dying in bed's the ticket — providing you're alone when it happens. Cashing in because of a woman — dying with a skirt for a blindfold — that kind of death is for suckers."

(*During the above,* SECOND ORDERLY *enters.* FIRST ORDERLY *puts a cigarette to his lips from the*

> *pack, offers one to the* SECOND, *who strikes a*
> *kitchen match on the gurney, near* STONE'*s head,*
> *to light both cigarettes*)

SECOND ORDERLY:   Who's this one?

FIRST ORDERLY:   Stone. Something Stone. Bought a bullet
in the shoulder.

SECOND ORDERLY:   He gonna make it?

FIRST ORDERLY:   Private dick. No great loss if he don't.
> (*As flashback effect begins and* STONE *is wheeled*
> *off*)

OOLIE'S VOICE (*Offstage, filtered*):   Stone Investigations,
Miss Oolie speaking.

STONE'S VOICE (*Offstage, filtered*):   We get any busier, you
can start reading *two* newspapers.

OOLIE'S VOICE (*Offstage, filtered*):   Yesterday's lies with today's date on 'em. Happy Monday.

STONE'S VOICE (*Offstage, filtered, after a beat*):   Was it only
Monday?
> (*A phone rings offstage*)
Can your whole life roll over and play dead, turn bad-side
out in just seven days?
> (*The phone rings again. Flashback effect ends*)

*Scene 2*

INT.    STONE'S OUTER OFFICE — DAY

> OOLIE, STONE's *secretary, at her desk, stops reading her newspaper and answers her phone.*

OOLIE:    Stone Investigations, Miss Oolie speaking ... No, he's not, can I help you? ... It's a flat rate. Twenty-five dollars a day plus eight cents a mile ... I'm sorry your wife's cheating on you, mister, but there's no discount for veterans.
> (*She hangs up and begins to read her newspaper. A beat, then the door opens and* STONE *enters. As he hangs up his coat and hat:*)

STONE:    Did I hear a phone?

OOLIE:    Some clown hoping for a few snaps of the little woman getting floor burns in the back of the family Chevy. I think he used a slug to pay for the call.

STONE:    We get any busier, you can start reading *two* newspapers.

OOLIE:    Yesterday's lies with today's date on 'em. Happy Monday.

STONE:    No such animal.
> (*Lights down on* OOLIE, *as lights up on* STONE's *private office.* STONE *enters, takes a whiskey bottle*

*from a file cabinet. As he looks through the blinds
at the street below:)*

STONE'S VOICE (*Over*): "Three million people in the City of Angels according to the last census, easily half of them up to something they don't want the other half to know. We all get sucked in by the lobby. Palm trees finger the sky and there's enough sunshine to lay some off on Pittsburgh. But that's all on top. L.A., truth to tell's, not much different than a pretty girl with the clap."
*(He tears a page off his desk calendar)*
"Monday. What other day works so hard at reminding you not to get your hopes up 'cause it's gonna be coming around again real soon?"
*(He crumples the page and tosses it into the wastebasket. The door opens and* OOLIE *enters excitedly; closes the door)*

OOLIE: Breakfast is over. Some business just walked in.
*(Corking the booze)*
And she's wearing a whole year's salary.

STONE (*Stashing the bottle*): A woman.

OOLIE: No flies on you.
*(Opens the door, addresses someone offstage)*
Mr. Stone'll see you now.
*(A moment, then* ALAURA *enters, a vision all in white)*
Alaura Villiers. Mr. Stone.
*(OOLIE exits, closing the door)*

ALAURA (*Sitting*): I know how busy you must be, Mr. Stone. I appreciate your seeing me.

(STONE *says nothing, just looks her over, as:*)

STONE'S VOICE (*Over*): "The appreciation was all mine. Just one look and you knew Alaura Villiers was a handful. Maybe two, if you played your cards right. She had the kind of face a man could hang a dream on, a body that made the Venus Di Milo look all thumbs, and only the floor kept her legs from going on forever."

(ALAURA *has taken a cigarette from a case. As* STONE *applies his lighter to it:*)

STONE: Can I be of some help, Mrs. Villiers?

ALAURA (*Correcting him*): Miss.

STONE: *Miss* Villiers.

ALAURA: I don't know where to begin.

STONE: Why don't you start by telling me if your husband knows you're running around town pretending to be single?

ALAURA: What makes you think I'm married?

STONE: When you slipped your ring off, you forgot how tan you are everywhere else. Or, at least, I imagine you are everywhere else. You want to tell me who you really are, now that we've established who you're not?

ALAURA: I'm in trouble, Mr. Stone.

STONE: Everyone is. It's only the smart ones who know it.

ALAURA: I'm really the last person in the world you'd expect in this kind of office. I've led a life I'd really think you could call dull. At least, I thought so until —
(*As she continues to speak words we do not hear:*)

STONE (*Sings*):
Just watch her dodge the truth like a runaway streetcar.
This role she plays could win her a prize.
Each gesture is correct,
Well chosen for effect,
And it would be wiser if I kept my eyes off her thighs.

ALAURA (*Spoken*): Mr. Stone? Are you listening to me?

STONE: I will, if you will — start leveling.

ALAURA: I beg your pardon?

STONE: Telling the truth. From the minute you walked in here, every time our eyes meet, you look like a deer caught in my headlights.

ALAURA: Let's just say I've been sizing you up.

STONE: All the measurements fit?

ALAURA: This is a very delicate situation, Mr. Stone. Reputations are at stake.

STONE: We don't share that problem.

ALAURA: My name is Alaura Kingsley. Mrs. Alaura Kingsley. My daughter, Mallory, is missing. Stepdaughter, actually. My husband is a good deal older than I am.

STONE: How *good* a deal?

ALAURA: He's seventy-five. I know how that must sound, but we're very much in love. Mallory's disappearance has been devastating to my husband.
(*Hands him a snapshot*)
He's just not the same when she's not around. It's as though part of him has gone off somewhere. The secret,

tender part.

     *(Re snapshot)*

She was sixteen then.

STONE:  An early developer.

ALAURA:  It's not a terribly good picture.

STONE *(Returning it)*:  I don't know if I could stand a better one.

ALAURA:  You won't need it?

STONE:  Or this case, Mrs. Kingsley. I've been around the block enough times to already feel myself getting a black-jack facial somewhere down the line, or having someone use my ribs for a shoe rack. You get to trust your instincts after awhile —

     *(As he continues, soundlessly:)*

ALAURA *(Sings)*:

This song and dance of his is most unconvincing.

He has that hungry look in his eye.

He needs the work, and soon,

Some cash'll change his tune.

He'll hop to the task,

I'll say jump and he'll

Ask me how high.

STONE *(Spoken)*:  So thanks, Mrs. Kingsley, but no thanks all the same.

   *(He opens the door, indicating the interview is over)*

ALAURA *(Producing her checkbook)*:  Shall we say a hundred dollars now, over and above whatever it finally comes to?

  *(STONE closes the door. As ALAURA writes a check:)*

STONE (*Sings*):
> This job is not to be believed,
> And I do not believe a word.
> Between her double talk and all that's unsaid
> I'd bet the farm that there'll be trouble ahead.

> I might be willingly deceived
> 'Cause I can trust myself around her
> Even less than I trust her
> But even so, I need the dough.

ALAURA (*Spoken, handing him the check*):   There'll be a considerable bonus when you find her. How considerable will surprise you.

STONE:   You're talking "when," I'm thinking "if."

ALAURA (*Standing, handing him* MALLORY's *photo*):   My money's on you. You look like the kind of man who can get the job done.

STONE:   You want to give me your unlisted number or do I just dial every possible combination?

ALAURA:   It would be better if you didn't call. I'll check with you.

STONE:   Why'd I get the nod, Mrs. Kingsley?
> (*Opening the door*)
> You can't swing a dead cat over your head in this town without hitting a private investigator.

ALAURA:   No special reason. I saw your name in the phone book.
> (*They exit his office, enter his outer office.* OOLIE, *at her desk, stares at* ALAURA's *check in* STONE's *hand*)

STONE (*To* ALAURA):   "Stone" have a certain ring to it?
(ALAURA *laughs*)
My secretary will see you out. Miss Oolie.

OOLIE (*Opening the door*):   Miss Villiers.

ALAURA (*A goodbye*):   Mr. Stone.

STONE:   Mrs. Kingsley.

ALAURA (*Exiting*):   Good day.
(OOLIE *closes the door after her, then turns to* STONE)

OOLIE:   She get married while she was in there?

STONE:   Her husband's name slipped her mind.

OOLIE:   It can happen, I guess.
(*We hear the sound of a typewriter and* STINE *appears, working at his desk.* OOLIE *and* STONE *speak their last three lines backwards and move in the same fashion to their previous positions, then freeze.* ALAURA *backs into the room, says her "Good day" backwards, and also freezes.* STINE *thinks a moment. When he types again:*)

ALAURA (*Exiting*):   Good day.

OOLIE (*Closes the door; then to* STONE):   She get married while she was in there?

STONE:   Her husband's name slipped her mind. He's seventy-five.

OOLIE:   There's probably not much else he slips her.
(*They laugh.* STINE *indicates his dissatisfaction and strikes his X key several times.* STONE *and*

> OOLIE, *totally unaware of* STINE'*s presence, speak*
> *their last three lines backwards and move in the*
> *same fashion to their previous positions. They*
> *freeze.* STINE *resumes typing:*)

STONE:  Her husband's name slipped her mind. He's seventy-five.

OOLIE:  He must've decided to go out with a bang instead of a whimper.
> (STONE *hands her* ALAURA'*s check*)
It's been a long time —
> (*A phone rings.* OOLIE *stops talking, as* STINE *stops typing. When he resumes:*)
— since I've seen two zeros —
> (*Another ring interrupts* STINE'*s typing and* OOLIE'*s speech. When* STINE *types again:*)
— next to each other.
> (*Annoyed,* STINE *stops typing, lifts his receiver*)

STINE:  Yes?
> (*Lights down on* STONE *and* OOLIE. *Lights remain up on* STINE, *as others come up on:*)

### Scene 3

BUDDY FIDLER's *office. An elderly* SHOESHINE BOY *polishing his shoes,* BUDDY *speaks into one of his three phones.*

BUDDY:  Stine? Buddy.

STINE:  Buddy!

BUDDY:  I just got your first pages. I was going to read 'em tonight, but I couldn't wait.

STINE:  And now you wish you had?

BUDDY:  Sweetheart, I'm your biggest fan. I've read a synopsis of every book you've ever written. With a little mustard on some rye, every word is a meal. But nothing was ever hurt by being improved.

STINE:  Let me get the pages.

BUDDY:  Get the pages.
(*As* STINE *looks for the script pages, sings*)
I buy a book and I get stuck with the author;
You buy a rose you're stuck with a thorn.
It's undeniable —
The guy is pliable,
And Shakespeare and Dickens were washed up before I was born.

STINE (*Having found the pages*):  Buddy? Shoot.

BUDDY:  Alright, alright, I gotta be honest, no matter how much it hurts me. I just didn't expect you to go into business for yourself, y'know what I mean? Those three shots in the dark, then opening in the hospital, Stone being wheeled in. We never said the rest of the picture was going to be a flashback. Not once in all these weeks. I mean, the main titles, then boom! right into a flashback? That's kicked. It's tired. Flashbacks are a thing of the past. Anyway, we're gonna do one later, when we show Stone with his girl, the nightclub singer —

STINE:  Bobbi.

BUDDY:  Bobbi, right, back in their early days, aren't we?
        (*Another of his phones rings*)

STINE:  But the book started with a flashback.

BUDDY:  Don't go 'way.
        (*Picking up second phone*)
        Yeah, put him on . . .
        (*Hanging up second phone, picking up third*)
        Henry? Henry, look, never mind it's perfect. We gotta take out four minutes.
        (*As* STINE *pours a whiskey:*)
        Nothing any good's ever hurt by cutting — circumcisions to one side, of course.
        (SHOESHINE BOY *laughs,* BUDDY *joins in. Then, into third phone:*)
        It's all in how who does it. I could take ten seconds out of "The Minute Waltz," and nobody'd ever know.
        (*Into first phone*)
        Hang on, babe.

        (*Into third phone*)

Did you recut the scene where the puppy dies?
> (*To* SHOESHINE BOY)

Just a little darker.
> (*Into third phone*)

How much time did that save?
> (*To* SHOESHINE BOY)

Beautiful.
> (*Into third phone*)

Great. Call me when you make the other cuts. Beautiful.
> (*Hanging up third phone, into first*)

I *know* the book started with a flashback. If I wanted to just shoot the book, I'd take pictures of the pages and save a fortune on actors. Just do it like we agreed, alright? Open with Oolie answering the phone, bring in Stone, then in comes Alaura Kingsley asking him to look for Mallory. And in the future, you gotta promise to do me one favor I insist on. After we agree on something, don't try to make it better. Donna tell you the car'll pick you up early? I'm screening two pictures, so I want to start a little sooner.
> (*To* SHOESHINE BOY)

That's too dark. There's dark and there's dark.

STINE: I'm coming alone. Gabby's publisher wants her back in New York.

BUDDY: Can't she go tomorrow? I'm showing the new Sturges.

STINE: She's a little harder to rewrite than I am.

BUDDY: That's all I need, you missing her right now. You're not the same when your wife's not around, you know that?
> (*Glancing at* STINE'S *pages*)

33

It's like part of you's gone off somewhere. The secret, tender part. Tell her to haul her fanny back here soon. I'm the only one gets to make you unhappy, right? I need the new pages first thing yesterday. I'm going to open my window — I want to see some fingers flying. Stine? Let me hear a smile.

                (STINE *smiles despite himself*)

Louder!

                (*A laugh from* STINE)

That's my boy!

                (*Lights down on* BUDDY)

STINE (*Hangs up, sings*):
This job is not to be believed,
And I cannot believe my luck.
I'm at the literary prime of my life
And I'm about to have the time of my life.
Unless I'm easily deceived,
Though Buddy doesn't tend to sugarcoat his comments,
He's all right,
All bark, no bite.

I've always longed for a chance to be watching
A book of my own on the screen.
To look up and see Stone on the screen
Would be better than fine.
Sit with my wife in a crowd
As the credits are shown on the screen,
In a frame all alone on the screen
It says, "Screenplay by Stine."

For making movies out of books
They say that Buddy wrote the book.
I can depend on him to give me some lip,

But you can trust a guy who shoots from the hip.
Out here, where nothing's how it looks,
It's hard to disregard a candid stand-up guy
Who skips the double talk
And lets you know exactly what he's thinking about you.
And I can beat the odds
And meet his demands,
Though I'm a stranger in
This strangest of lands.

This mad adventure I've begun
Is unlike anything I know.
It's gonna be a lotta work
And lots of fun
And pots of dough.
> (*He resumes typing, reactivating* STONE *and* OOLIE)

*Scene 4*

**RESUME STONE'S OUTER OFFICE — DAY**

STONE *and* OOLIE *still stare at* ALAURA's *check.*

STONE:   Go straight to the bank and cash it. Take out three weeks pay for yourself.

OOLIE:   You only owe me for two.

STONE:   Grab it while you can, kid.
(*As he puts on his hat and coat:*)

OOLIE:   Good looking woman, Mrs. What's-her-names.

STONE:   I didn't notice.

OOLIE:   I noticed how much you didn't. What's her problem? Her husband got a little something on the side?

STONE:   The man's seventy-five.

OOLIE:   Some guys'll crawl out of the grave to cheat.
(*Seeing* MALLORY's *snapshot in his hand*)
Runaway daughter?

STONE:   If that was you, where would I find you?

OOLIE:   Probably in front of a mirror.

STONE (*Studying the photo*):   Some kind of prime, huh?

OOLIE:   I didn't notice.

STONE: Young and ripe.

OOLIE: She'll get over it. We're all that for about thirty seconds.

STONE: Step-mama didn't.

OOLIE: She didn't altogether leave, did she?

STONE: That kind never does.
(*He starts to exit, freezes in the open door. Lights up on:*)

*Scene 5*

STINE's *bedroom at the Garden of Allah.* STINE *dresses, as his wife,* GABBY, *packs a suitcase.*

STINE: Isn't there any way you could do whatever editing you have to do out here?

GABBY (*Shrugs*): Your work takes you away from home, my work takes me back.

STINE: Can I be perfectly honest?

GABBY: Can honesty be *im*perfect?

STINE: I don't think you mind going back to New York at all.

GABBY: I can't deny I prefer working face-to-face with authors who *are* the authors of their work.

STINE: Am I about to be insulted, or has it already happened?

GABBY: That contract, your contract, just sticks in my craw.

STINE: Gabby, it's a standard clause.

GABBY: That the *studio* is the author of the screenplay? That after writing the script you're writing, it turns out you never wrote it at all?

STINE: If it's good enough for Faulkner and Fitzgerald —

GABBY: Then it's bad enough for you. Darling, for five thousand a week, you're willing to be as much of a hired hand as Stone is. You really should ask for eight cents a mile, too.

STINE: Five times ten weeks is fifty thousand dollars. Fifty thousand times three pictures is a *hundred* and fifty thousand dollars.

GABBY: Is there *ever* a conversation out here where anyone's at a loss for numbers? Do you have any idea what all that money is costing you? He thinks of writers as overpaid typists, Buddy does.

STINE: You've got him wrong, Gab.

GABBY: You see the glass half full.

STINE: And you see him peeing into it.
> (*Taking her arm*)
I can take care of myself. I can do it even better when you're doing it for me.
> (*A car horn offstage*)

GABBY: My taxi.

STINE: Studio car. Buddy's disappointed you're not coming to the screening, you know.

GABBY: He'll get over it. He got over not being God. I'm sure there'll be someone nice there you can watch his picture show with.

STINE (*Embracing her*): I don't want anyone nice. I want you.

GABBY (*A beat*): I'll know, you know. No one'll have to say anything. I'll know; the way I did last time.

STINE:   Last time was the last time. That's the truth.

GABBY:   The truth? The truth to you, sad to say, is whatever works for the moment. It's something that holds up two times in a row.

(*Car horn*)

STINE:   I'll miss you.

(*A kiss, then:*)

GABBY:   When are you going to start liking yourself a little more so you can stand for people to like you a little less?

STINE (*Smiles*):   I'll call.

GABBY:   I'd rather you wrote. Anything but what you're writing.

(STINE *exits.* STONE *exits his office, simultaneously*)

## *Scene 6*

> GABBY, *in her set;* OOLIE, *alone in* STONE's *outer office, sing.*

GABBY:
What you don't know about women

OOLIE:
What you don't know about women

BOTH:
Could fill a shelf of books.

GABBY:
You are the type of man who looks
For understanding lovers

OOLIE:
But never understands the girl
Who lies beneath the covers.

BOTH:
You only have to open up your mouth to show

GABBY:
What you don't know

OOLIE:
And you don't know

BOTH:
About women.

A woman needs to be assured
That she remains alluring,
To now and then be reassured
Your passion is enduring.

GABBY:

It's not enough to know your line
To polish and routine it

OOLIE:

And heaven knows I know your line,
The whole routine, I've seen it.

BOTH:

Ya gotta mean it.

GABBY:

What you don't know about women

OOLIE:

What you don't know about women

BOTH:

Is what we need to hear.

GABBY:

You think if you can sound sincere
Then we'll come running to you.

OOLIE:

Throw in some truth for atmosphere
But we can see right through you.

GABBY:

And ev'ry hollow compliment and phrase defines

OOLIE:

And underlines

BOTH:
> What you don't know about women.
>
> You think what I don't know will not hurt me,
> But you don't know how often you do.
> How long ago did good sense desert me?
> I don't know why I still burn for you.

GABBY:
> You're immature and shortsighted,

OOLIE:
> You're an incurable player,

GABBY:
> You show a lack of discretion,

OOLIE:
> You don't know jack about heartache,

GABBY:
> You're out of sync with your feelings,

OOLIE:
> You only wink at commitment,

GABBY:
> You're running low on emotion.

BOTH:
> What you don't know about women's
> Only a drop in the ocean
> Next to what you don't know about me.
>
> You are in need of
> A little enlight'ning
> On ladies and love
> But you can't see,

## CITY OF ANGELS

What you don't know about women
Is fright'ning
And you don't know nothin' about me.
                    (*Blackout*)

*Scene* 7

INT.   STONE'S PLACE — NIGHT

*A dreary bungalow — the only brightness coming from the radio.*

RADIO ANNOUNCER'S VOICE:   From Hollywood and Vine, entertainment capitol of the world, it's the "Hour of Powers" — featuring the song stylings of America's favorite balladeer — Jimmy Powers!
   (*As radio orchestra hits "Stay with Me,"* STONE, *in shirt sleeves, appears from his bathroom off-stage, wiping a dinner plate. He crosses to the stove, opens a can of food and empties it into a pot on one of the burners*)

STONE'S VOICE (*Over*):   "The rent's forty-two-fifty a month at the Beverly Cresta Court. No one I know's got a clue who Beverly was, but they named half of everything in L.A. after her. My neighbor on one side was a minister at a pet cemetery, who also answered fan mail for Gene Autry; on the other, someone with half a brow who advertised, 'Income Tax Returns and High Colonics While You Wait.' Life at the Beverly Cresta could be exceedingly dull — a fact I was often too dumb to appreciate."
   (STONE *takes* MALLORY's *photo from his jacket, studies it and tosses it on the bed. On studio applause from the radio:*)

JIMMY'S VOICE (*Offstage, filtered*): Thank you, thank you, thank you. And now, a wonderful Del DaCosta tune I introduced in my movie, "Three Guys Named Joe." "Ya Gotta Look Out for Yourself!" Hit it, Bernie!

ANGEL CITY 4'S VOICES (*Sing, filtered*):
Look out,
Look out,
Look out for yourself!
(*A knock on* STONE's *door*)

MAN'S VOICE (*Offstage, behind the door*): Mr. Stone?

STONE: Yeah?

MAN'S VOICE: Special delivery for Mr. Stone.

STONE: Slip it under the door.

MAN'S VOICE: Ya gotta sign for it.

STONE (*Turns the radio down*): Slip the pencil under, too.
(*A beat, then the door crashes into the room, knocked off its hinges by* BIG SIX, *a mountain of a man. His partner,* SONNY, *is small, but just as menacing*)

SONNY (*To* STONE): Ya got a lot to learn about being a host, friend. How'd ya like it if we slipped *you* under the door?
(*He dips a finger into the pot and tastes its contents. Then, to* STONE)
This needs salt.

STONE: Who sent you guys? Duncan Hines?

SONNY: Big Six here would like a word with ya.

STONE: I'm all ears.

SONNY:   Ya don't need 'em. He talks with his hands.

STONE (*Turning, to hit* BIG SIX):   Is that so — ?
    (BIG SIX *knocks* STONE *to the floor*)

BIG SIX (*To* SONNY):   Hope this don't disturb the neighbors.

SONNY:   Yeah. Let's give 'em a little music.
    (*He turns the radio up;* JIMMY POWERS *and*
    ANGEL CITY 4 *appear in a radio studio set. As*
    STONE *is administered a terrible beating by* BIG
    SIX *and* SONNY, *the radio set moves across the
    stage, obscuring the action in the bungalow, which
    is projected in shadows on* STONE's *ceiling*)

JIMMY & ANGEL CITY 4 (*Sing*):
    Ya gotta look out for yourself,
    If you're hoping to be first,
    Then ya better think "Me first,"
    Or you're gonna finish last.

    Ya gotta look out for yourself,
    If you follow this format,
    You'll be nobody's doormat,
    It's a rule that's hard and fast.

    This world ain't pure,
    On this you can depend,
    You best be sure
    That you're your own best friend.

    Ya gotta look out for yourself,
    If you're planning to do good,
    Then be sure it does you good,
    You don't wanna be too good.

    Ya gotta look out for yourself,

Ya know the score when you adore yourself,
When you're in danger you can count on me to shout —
Look out for yourself.
(*As music continues:*)

SONNY (*Spoken, to the barely conscious* STONE): Lemme give you a message, Mr. Stone: Drop the Kingsley case, y'unnerstan'? Drop it, or next time we'll have to get rough. Sorry we kept ya from your dinner. An' take my word for it . . .
(*Yanking* STONE's *head back by his hair*)
It needs more salt.
(*To* BIG SIX, *letting* STONE's *head collapse*)
How 'bout a cuppa joe?

BIG SIX: Gotta get somepin' for my girl's birthday.

SONNY: She got a radio?

BIG SIX: No.

SONNY: Here. Give 'er this.
(SONNY *yanks the radio free of the wall, bringing the music and the sight of* JIMMY POWERS *and the* ANGEL CITY 4 *to an abrupt end.* SONNY *tosses the radio to* BIG SIX)

BIG SIX (*Pleased*): Yeah.
(*He exits.* SONNY *collects his coat and hat and exits, singing a few bars of "Ya Gotta Look Out for Yourself." As lights dim on the crumpled* STONE:)

STONE'S VOICE (*Over*): "It was as though I'd been hit by a wrecking ball wearing a pinkie ring. Some part of me that still seemed to be functioning was watching the other part of me that wasn't, fall. Then, that part started falling, too,

and the race began to see which part could hit bottom
first . . ."
   (*As* STONE'S *voice fades,* BUDDY'S *takes over. Fade
   out on* STONE)

## Scene 8

BUDDY's *office.* BUDDY, *having a haircut, is read-ing screenplay pages aloud to* GILBERT, *his barber.*

BUDDY:   " . . . Somehow I was getting the idea that this was God's way of punishing me for having a hundred dollars all at once."

GILBERT:   Is that supposed to be funny?

BUDDY:   Half-and-half.

GILBERT:   It's about right, then.

BUDDY:   Donna! Waiting is expensive.
(DONNA *enters — the same actress who plays* OOLIE)

DONNA:   He's on his way.

BUDDY:   Here would be even better. That dress is half an inch too long. It'll photograph even longer.

DONNA:   I'm not in a movie.

BUDDY:   Everybody's in a movie. Sometimes we just turn the camera on.
(*Looking at pages*)
You can tell a writer every time. Words, words, words, that's all they know. This could take awhile. Who've I got for lunch?

DONNA:  Carla.

BUDDY (*Engrossed in pages*):  Who?

DONNA:  Your wife.

BUDDY:  Cancel her.

DONNA:  One or two dozen?

BUDDY:  Whichever's more.
(*Looking in mirror*)
Beautiful. The man's an artist.
(*To* GILBERT, *affectionately*)
Took me long enough to teach you.

GILBERT:  See you tomorrow, Mr. Fidler.
(*He exits, as* STINE *enters*)

STINE:  Knock, knock?

BUDDY:  The man of my dreams. I just got the pages where Stone gets beat up.

STINE:  You like 'em?

BUDDY:  Like is for pishers. These are to love. They're perfect.
(*Laughs*)
But we'll fix 'em.

STINE:  Can't I finish the script before we fix it?

BUDDY:  Sure, you can finish it, but first, we'll fix.

STINE:  What is it, you want new words?

BUDDY:  No, no, no. There're too many words now. Give me pictures. Paint me scenes. Movies are shadows. They're light, they're dark. They're faces ten feet high.

Close-up of him! Close-up of her! Cut to close-up of husband watching close-up of her watching close-up of him!
(*Beat*)
You'll get it, you'll see. Sweetheart, nobody gets a hole-
in-one their first time at bat. There's people make a fortune writing movies, and *they* don't know how. I mean, no
offense, everybody and his brother writes books, but a
screenplay . . .

STINE: That's a ballgame of a different color, right?

BUDDY: When Buddy Fidler talks, you're not listening to
someone else.
(*Sings*)

You're a literary great
Who should've won a Pulitzer prize,
I would never cannibalize
Or impair a single hair or phrase
Of your amazing opus.
Still a lot of scribblers
Soon discover what they write for the screen
Isn't always right for the screen,
So I intervene.

I'm not gonna give you a lecture
'Cause, Stine, I respect yer craft,
But spare me a sec and
You'll spare us the *drek*,
Such as this second rate second draft.

'Cause ev'rything goes for the visual,
You don't need much prose for the visual.
You send in the pros for the visual,
And I have a nose for the visual.

I've got twelve nominations, a half dozen Oscars,
Nine cars and three ex-wives to show
That in this business of refuse and nephews
I know my stuff.

I zipped through your book
And the characters jumped to life on the page,
Now we're at the stage
Where I bring them to life on the screen.
Don't cling to the words to which you gave birth,
Remember how many a picture is worth,
The odds are a thousand to one so get used to it, Stine,
The book may be yours, baby, trust me the movie is mine.

Ya learn from Von Sternberg,
Ya grow from Von Stroheim,
And so I'm the heir to their skill.
This town has more nuts than Brazil
Let's face it, I've been through DeMille.

Don't balk, be like Faulkner,
A *mensch* just like Benchley.
Essent'lly they hand you the plot;
For writers I liked 'em a lot.
I used to get plotzed with F. Scott.

Authors unprepared to take
A stab at this collab'rative art
Must suppress their egos and part
With the notion that in motion pictures
Words are carved in marble.
Donna, darling, get this on a pad
And type it up for next week;
I have an engagement to speak
At the Writers Guild.

You wouldn't want to upset Buddy
This is advice not a threat, buddy
But see how tough things can get, buddy
When things get rough it can get bloody
Baby, nobody says no, Buddy,
So, buddy, you better concede
Let Buddy be Buddy
Pure Buddy
And he'll be your buddy
The buddy you need.
    (*Spoken, to* DONNA, *having waltzed* STINE *off-stage, his script pages in hand*)
Next!
                (*Blackout*)

## *Scene 9*

**INT. STONE'S PLACE — LATER**

> STONE, *still unconscous, lies atop his bed. His ring-*
> *ing phone is answered by* LT. MUNOZ, *a plain-*
> *clothes detective.*

MUNOZ:   Oolie? What do you say, sweetheart? . . . Right.
It's Manny Munoz . . .
> *(A glance at* STONE)

Looks to me like he's out right now. Can I tell him anything for you? . . . Thanks, I love you, too, muchacha.
> *(He hangs up, as his assistant,* PASCO, *a uniformed*
> *policeman, enters from the bathroom and slowly*
> *pours the contents of a water glass on* STONE's
> *bloodied face, bringing him around)*

Stone? You alright?

STONE:   How'd you get in here?

MUNOZ:   Not too tough when there's no door.

STONE:   You got a warrant?

MUNOZ:   Don't need one when the peace gets this dis-
turbed. Who did it?

STONE:   Did what?

MUNOZ:   Rearrange your furniture.

STONE:   Interior decorator.

MUNOZ:   He do your face, too? Neighbors said the whole place shook.

STONE:   Must've been an earthquake.

MUNOZ:   In just your bungalow?

STONE:   Nature's funny. Which one of you stole my radio?

MUNOZ:   What case you working on?

STONE:   Who says I am?

MUNOZ:   I see groceries.

STONE:   I got lucky on a quiz show.

MUNOZ:   How'd you like to win thirty days in the can for not answering?
(*As* STONE *looks at his beat-up reflection in the side of his toaster:*)

STONE:   Routine job. Same old kind of thing.

MUNOZ:   I forget. What old kind of thing would that be?

STONE:   I forget, too.

MUNOZ:   You're gonna need stitches, amigo. A lot, I hope.

STONE:   With a rusty needle, maybe.

PASCO:   Makes my mouth water.

STONE (*Applying a kitchen towel to his wounds*):   Take your dog for a walk, Lieutenant. I don't want him messing my carpet.

MUNOZ:   Whatever you're up to, six-to-five there's a dame

in the picture.

STONE:   Gambling's illegal.

PASCO (*Handing* MUNOZ MALLORY's *photo*):   Lieutenant.

MUNOZ (*Smiling at photo*):   More like even money.
(*To* PASCO)
Ten years I know this guy. We pounded the same beat together. There's never been a dame couldn't twist him around her finger from a block away.
(*Laughing,* MUNOZ *and* PASCO *start to leave. The flashback effect begins*)

STONE'S VOICE (*Over*):   "Munoz was right. Me and dames. Shorthand for trouble. Beginning with Bobbi."
(*Beat*)
"Bobbi."
(*Her name still hurts*)
"Whoever said 'Time heals all wounds' never knew anyone like Bobbi."

*Scene 10*

**INT.  THE BLUE NOTE — A  COCKTAIL  LOUNGE — NIGHT**

MAN'S VOICE (*Over, filtered*):  Ladies and gentlemen, the
Blue Note proudly presents the sultry song stylings of —
Miss Bobbi Edwards.
> (*The small* CROWD *applauds. The sultry singer is*
> BOBBI *— the same actress who plays* GABBY)

BOBBI (*Sings*):
There's not a morning that I open up my eyes
And find I didn't dream of you,
Without a warning, though it's never a surprise,
Soon as I awake
Thoughts of you arise
With ev'ry breath I take.

At any time
Or place
I close my eyes and see your face
And I'm
Embracing you.
If only I believed that dreams come true.

Darling,
You were the one who said forever from the start
And I've been drifting since you've gone,
Out on a lonely sea that only you can chart.

I've been going on
Knowing that my heart will break
With ev'ry breath I take.
> (STONE *and* MUNOZ, *as young police officers, enter.* MUNOZ *takes a stool at the bar. Music continuing,* STONE *takes* BOBBI's *hand*)

STONE (*Spoken*):   Bobbi . . .

BOBBI:   I've still got half a chorus to do.

STONE:   Do it engaged.
> (*Slipping a ring on her finger*)
Not a word. Only "yes."
> (*As they dance:*)

BOBBI:   Sweetheart, you know I can't. Not yet.

STONE:   Come on, babe. They'd have to make a million movies a year to get in everybody wants to be a star.

BOBBI:   Irwin S. Irving's coming by next Monday. There's nobody bigger in the business. If he likes me, it could be my chance. My chance to be somebody.

STONE:   I figured you for that already.

BOBBI:   Can't you just see me?

STONE:   All I can see — all I want to see — is us.
> (BOBBI *returns to the mike*)

BOBBI (*Sings*):
You were the one who said forever from the start
And I've been drifting since you've gone,
Out on a lonely sea that only you can chart.
I've been going on
Knowing that my heart will break

With ev'ry breath I take.
  (PATRONS *applaud.* BOBBI *bows and exits. The
  lights fade*)

## Scene 11

FADE IN:    INT.    THE BLUE NOTE — BACKSTAGE
— ANOTHER NIGHT

*Lights up on dressing room door as* STONE *enters.*

STONE'S VOICE (*Over*):    "Monday nights I was usually too
busy to drop by to see Bobbi. And she knew it."

STONE (*Knocks on the door*):    Bobbi.
            (*No response*)
Bobbi!
            (*It's locked*)
Open up, God damn it! Open it!
    (*He shoulders the door open, enters the dark room*)

STONE'S VOICE (*Over*):    "If there really is someplace called
Hell, the calendar's nothing but Monday's."
    (*He turns on the light, sees a man's empty trouser
    leg on the floor, the balance of the trousers behind
    the curtain that is drawn on the room's bed. He
    pulls the curtain aside, to reveal* IRWIN S. IRVING
    — *the same actor who plays* BUDDY FIDLER — *in-
    stantly panicked at being caught in the act with a
    scantily-clad* BOBBI)

IRWIN:    Who is this crazy maniac?
            (*Quickly*)

Don't call the police!

STONE:    I *am* the police, you son-of-a-bitch!

IRWIN:    No one calls Irwin S. Irving a son-of-a-bitch to his face! You know how much I gave to charity last year?

STONE (*To* BOBBI, *drawing his gun*):    This is how you get in the movies? He bring his own casting couch with him?

IRWIN (*Indicating his pants*):    My left pocket! There's thousands in there! Take it all! This never happened!
(STONE *points the gun at him, frightening him further*)
How would you like to be in my next picture?

STONE (*Ready to hit him*):    Why you —

BOBBI (*Trying to restrain* STONE):    No! Don't!
(*There is a three-way scuffle. As bodies collide against the make-up table, all the lights go off. In the darkness:*)

IRWIN'S VOICE:    Are you nuts?! You're not trying to shoot just anyone here, you know! Stop! For God's sake, stop him!
(*Two gunshots are heard.* BOBBI *screams. A cry of pain from* IRWIN. *Blackout*)

## Scene 12

STINE's *office.*

STINE (*On the phone*):   No, no, no, it's going pretty well, Gab. I just finished Scene 17. The flashback of the shooting in Bobbi's dressing room. It's fine, I guess. Buddy's teaching me to write with guns instead of words. What do you think of this scene? A new one. Starts with a close-up of a writer missing his wife. Okay to cut to a close-up of her missing him? . . . Good. I'll print it. Talk to you tomorrow.
(*As he hangs up,* DONNA *enters, with script pages*)
Donna.

DONNA:   I don't mean to interrupt.

STINE (*Smiling*):   Then what good are you?

DONNA (*Handing him the pages*):   Buddy's been re-reading the new pages. I wanted to break the fall.

STINE:   Oh?

DONNA:   He doesn't like Irwin S. Irving getting shot.

STINE:   This morning he was in love with it.

DONNA:   One for the rule of thumb department: love is also something you fall out of.
(*As* STINE *crumples the pages into a ball*)
I don't think the scene's dead; he just wants to fix it.

STINE:  Funny, how he can keep doing this to people without taking his pants down.
>    (*He tosses her the balled paper*)

DONNA:  You're wicked. He *has* to recognize himself in Irwin S. Irving.

STINE:  People never see themselves as others write them. You see any of you in Oolie's character?

DONNA:  Me? Never!

STINE:  I rest my case.
>    (DONNA *puts the ball of paper on his desk and starts to go*)
>
> Donna.
>    (*He tosses her the ball*)
> Thanks for breaking the fall.

DONNA:  Just trying to be the best Oolie I can.
>    (*As she starts to go once more:*)

STINE:  Either of you ladies free for dinner tonight?

DONNA (*Exiting, smiling*):  Donna might be.
>    (STINE, *pleased, sits, reads what's in his type-writer*)

STINE:  "Scene 18. Exterior. Downtown L.A. Day. Overcast."
>    (*A public phone booth comes on, a* MAN *on the phone*)
> "Medium shot of a public phone booth at the corner of Sunset and Anywhere. The camera intrudes on one of the city's slimier angels, a rather smudged carbon copy of a human being, as he tries to set the record for a nickel's worth of heavy breathing. After establishing, Oolie enters."

(OOLIE *enters, waits at the booth*)
"As the creepy caller slithers off, Oolie wipes the receiver with the sleeve of her dress and places a call."
(OOLIE *does just that, as the* MAN *exits*)
"Cut to close-up of Oolie in mid-conversation."

OOLIE (*On the phone*): My teller friend at the bank recognized her signature. He told me who she was, he was so grateful to finally get a check from you that wouldn't hit the ceiling if he dropped it. Listen, you ever want to get in touch with Mrs. Kingsley, just try the top of Paso Robles Drive, right where it overlooks Arroyo Seco Canyon . . . I know. It doesn't get much more Pasadena than that. Looks like Mrs. Kingsley's not just any old Mrs. Kingsley, huh? Be careful. I'm getting that funny feeling I get in my bones, when people want to start breaking yours . . . Stone?

(*He has hung up. The pay phone goes off. The terrace of the Kingsley mansion appears*)

*Scene 13*

**EXT.   THE KINGSLEY MANSION — TERRACE — DAY**

ALAURA KINGSLEY, *in tennis togs, reclines on a chaise.* PETER KINGSLEY, *20-ish, also dressed for tennis, enjoys the job of oiling her bare legs.*

ALAURA:   Higher. Deeper.

PETER:   I don't want to hurt you.

ALAURA:   Don't be a killjoy.
(MARGARET, *a maid, enters*)

MARGARET:   Mrs. Kingsley, there's a Mr. Stone?

ALAURA:   Oh? Thank you, Margaret. I'll see him here.
(MARGARET *exits*)

PETER:   Stone? Here? So fast? Has there been some kind of change?

ALAURA:   Peter, let me think.

PETER:   Is there something I don't know?

ALAURA:   I'll make a list for you later, darling. In the meantime, you just let me handle Mr. Stone.

PETER:   You think everything's alright?

ALAURA:   I think you might just better finish my knee, Peter, and try acting natural — if you can somehow remember what that's like.

(*She lifts her leg for oiling. A beat, then* STONE *enters, a strip of adhesive over one eye, another on the bridge of his nose*)

Mr. Stone. What a pleasant treat.

STONE (*Observing the oiling*):   This seems to be your day for them.

ALAURA:   This is my stepson, Peter Kingsley. Peter, this is Mr. Stone.

PETER (*Wiping his oily hand*):   I'm afraid I'm a bit messy.

ALAURA:   We have to talk, darling. Why don't you warm up on the court and get ready for me?

PETER (*In leaving*):   Mr. Stone.

STONE (*To* ALAURA):   I don't know much about tennis, but how much more warming up you figure he needs?

ALAURA:   You don't play?

STONE:   Too hard at my place. I keep breaking the lamps.

ALAURA:   I didn't expect to see you so soon, Mr. Stone. Any leads on Mallory? Isn't that what you call them?

STONE:   I'm not here to teach you my business, Mrs. Kingsley. Just to tell you I don't want yours. I don't suppose you'd know why two trained apes showed up at my place last night to give me a crash course in bleeding?

ALAURA:   Your face —

STONE:   It'll live.

(*Handing her cash*)

That's your deposit, Mrs. Kingsley, minus twenty-five

dollars. I'm keeping a day's pay for the pounding. Only my friends beat me up for nothing.

ALAURA: I don't understand. Why would anyone not want Mallory found? I have no idea. That's the truth.

STONE: The truth! The truth to people like you, Mrs. Kingsley, is whatever works for the moment, something that can hold up two times in a row.

ALAURA: You're not out on the street now, Mr. Stone.

STONE: Give me five seconds. It was a treat seeing your home. It'll save me a trip to England.

ALAURA: I'm afraid you really can't quit, Mr. Stone. The choice isn't yours.

STONE: That'll be news to my logic.

ALAURA: My husband is not known for taking no for an answer. This way, please.

STONE'S VOICE (*Over*): "'This way, please.' Like she was leading me to Men's Sportswear."

(*As they make for the solarium*)

"Luther Kingsley. 'The Widow Maker.' Half the planes and tanks in World War Two were built by Luther Kingsley. There weren't too many stray millions the man didn't own. I say the man. He was more a shadow. Luther Kingsley hadn't been seen in public for years. Once he owned the world, he turned his back on it. Easy come, easy go, I guess.

## Scene 14

**INT.    THE KINGSLEY SOLARIUM — DAY**

*A sun-filled solarium. The doors of the room open for the entrance of* LUTHER KINGSLEY, *who has the head of a lion, which is all we see of him, for he is encased in an iron lung. Wheeling in the shiny cylinder is the impressive figure of* DR. MANDRIL. ALAURA *walks to* LUTHER, *whose face is reflected in a large mirror atop his life-sustaining machine.*

ALAURA (*Kissing* LUTHER's *brow*):    You look wonderful, darling.

MANDRIL:    Not too strenuous a visit, Alaura. We've done a lot of good, hard work this morning, haven't we, Luther?

ALAURA:    Doctor Mandril, this is Mr. Stone.

MANDRIL:    May I be of some service to you, sir?

STONE:    I'm told it's your patient I'm supposed to talk to.

MANDRIL:    Luther Kingsley is not my patient, sir. We are all cosmic voyagers. Luther Kingsley is my traveling companion. Infantile paralysis is tragic only to those who view it as a disease. I see it as but one of the many steps possible in the journey to the center of all truth.

ALAURA:    Dr. Mandril is my husband's spiritual therapist.

MANDRIL (*Arms held high, chants*):    Ommmm . . .

STONE:   Muscles for the soul.

MANDRIL:   Skepticism cures nothing, Mr. Stone.

STONE:   Fantasy even less.

LUTHER (*In a labored whisper*):   Stone! Find Mallory!

STONE:   Mr. Kingsley, last night two of nature's nastier mistakes tried out their recipe for face pudding on me so that I'd understand that the whereabouts of your daughter was no business of mine. Even with the one eye they didn't close, I could see their point. I've given your deposit back to your wife.

LUTHER:   Mandril!

MANDRIL:   Mr. Kingsley insists you reconsider.

STONE:   Mr. Kingsley, let me say this straight to your mirror, sir. No dice.

LUTHER:   Mandril!

MANDRIL:   Mr. Stone! If you do not agree to find Mallory, Mr. Kingsley will see to it that your investigator's license is held over a very slow flame at City Hall. You will be finished in this state.

STONE:   The country's got one or two more.

MANDRIL:   You can't see them, Mr. Stone —
                    (*Re iron lung*)
— but there are some very long fingers in there. Fingers that can reach wherever you go. Lest you feel Mr. Kingsley does not appreciate your possible jeopardy, Mrs. Kingsley spoke to you of a bonus? That figure is ten thousand dollars. We trust that won't take too much thinking about.

(*As* MANDRIL *wheels* LUTHER *off:*)

STONE'S VOICE (*Over*): "Ten thousand dollars. Next to Mrs. Kingsley's that was the best figure in the room."

STONE (*To* ALAURA): When was the last time you didn't get your way?

ALAURA (*Smiles*): You'll be the first to know.
(*She takes the cigarette from his lips and takes a drag*)

STONE: Nasty habit.

ALAURA: Only kind to have.
(*She returns the cigarette to his lips*)

STONE: Well, don't let me keep you.
(*Reminding her*)
Your tennis game.
(*Sings*)
You seem at home on the court.

ALAURA:
Let's say that I've played around.

STONE:
Well, you don't look like the sort.

ALAURA:
My hidden talents abound.
A competitor hasn't been found to defeat me.

STONE:
I'll bet you're a real good sport.

ALAURA:
Shall we say the ball is in your court?

STONE:
> I bet you like to play rough.

ALAURA:
> I like to work up a sweat.

STONE:
> And you just can't get enough.

ALAURA:
> I'm good for more than one set.
> But I promise I'll show no regret
> If you beat me.

STONE:
> My backhand is clearly my forte.

BOTH:
> Shall we say the ball is in your court?

ALAURA:
> No one *ever* plays with me.

STONE:
> I thought your next of kin did.

ALAURA:
> My husband *never* plays with me,
> He's too easily winded.

STONE:
> You leave me breathless, too.

ALAURA:
> Wait till our match is through.

STONE:
> I may lack form and finesse,
> But I'll warm up in a jiff.

ALAURA:
> It's not exciting unless
> The competition is stiff.

STONE:
> I think I understand your racquet,
> I'm not in your league.

ALAURA:
> But you can hack it.

STONE:
> This game commences with love.

ALAURA:
> Well, I think love is a bore.

STONE:
> Let's give the tempo a shove.

ALAURA:
> And raise the stakes a bit more.

BOTH:
> One thing I'm positive of:
> It's time for someone to score.

STONE:
> Tell me how you like to play.

ALAURA:
> On grass or clay
> And ev'ry day.

BOTH:
> They're both O.K.

ALAURA:
> But time is running short.
> Darling, let's don't dilly dally.

STONE:

Ready for a rousing rally.

BOTH:

Shall we say the ball is in your court?
(*The* BUTLER *appears to hand* STONE *his hat*)

STONE (*Spoken*):    It looks like one of us is leaving. I got the impression I was being asked to stay.

ALAURA:    *After* you find Mallory.

STONE:    The incentives never stop.

ALAURA:    I'm saving the best for last.
(*Sings*)
Shall we say the ball is in your court?
(*Blackout*)

## *Scene 15*

**EXT. THE SEARCH — DAY**

STONE'S VOICE (*Over*): "One more for the rule of thumb department: poor girls run away from home looking for something better, rich girls can't wait to find anything worse. With ten thousand and one new reasons to look for Mallory Kingsley, I started at the top, by going right to the bottom of the barrel."

> (ANGEL CITY 4, *dressed as low-lifes, enter and sing:*)

ANGEL CITY 4:
> On the loose and
> So elusive,
> You won't find her till you've checked
> Ev'ry avenue.
> Like a diamond
> In a coal mine,
> She's where you would least expect.
>
> Try to track her down,
> Go over the whole darn town.
> Go on a fishin'
> Expedition,
> Ev'rybody's gotta be somewhere.
>
> Girls don't vanish in thin air.

Ev'rybody's gotta be somewhere,
But where? Where? Where? Where?

Take a little looksee
Nose around,
There's an underground crowd to scout.
Use a little intuition if you wish
Your mission to pan out.
Keep an open ear and
Trust your gut,
Let the scuttlebutt cross your mind.
If you're out of innuendo 'round the bend
Are hints you've yet to find.

STONE:
Stay right on her trail.

ANGEL CITY ALTO:
This tomato is a hot potato.

STONE:
This case is a "beaut."

ANGEL CITY TENOR:
Dig deep and keep on diggin'.

STONE:
She's the Holy Grail.

ANGEL CITY SOPRANO:
She's a needle in haystack heaven.

STONE:
You're in hot pursuit,

ANGEL CITY ALTO & BARITONE:
You're warm and getting warmer.

ANGEL CITY 4:
> Don't be so low keyed,
> Start followin' ev'ry lead,
> Don't put your feet up,
> Turn the heat up,
> Ev'rybody's gotta be somewhere.
>
> Girls don't vanish in thin air.
> First ya gotta look left,
> Then ya gotta look right,
> Then ya better look high and low.
> Gotta run around town,
> Gotta play the old game,
> It's a little like tic tac toe.

STONE:
> Where's that dame?
> Where's she gone to?
> She's a flame
> That you're drawn to.
>
> Where, I wonder, am I gonna find this chick?
> It's quite a blunder to underestimate her.
> She's a stye in the eye of a private dick.
> She look familiar?

ANGEL CITY PORNO VENDOR:
> You don't know how many women I see each day
> Beneath innumerable guys.
> Yours would be hard to forget I regret to say
> She's one I never laid my eyes on.

STONE:
> Where I wonder am I gonna find this chick?
> It's quite a blunder to underestimate her.

> She's a stye in the eye of a private dick.
> She look familiar?

ANGEL CITY MADAM:
> Though I've never seen her,
> I've seen girls like this so young and ripe,
> Your missing miss is not the type
> To miss a misdemeanor.
> Why-doncha why-doncha why-doncha
> Let me choose a change of pace, for broads like this you
>    came
> To the right place.

STONE:
> Where's that dame?
> Where's she gone — ?

ANGEL CITY "B" GIRLS:
> You're quite a masterful detective,
> And it's your lucky day to stumble on us
> You'll find us a plus.
> It hardly seems at random.
> You're wise to scrutinize us,
> We won't refuse,
> So take off your shoes,
> We'll search for clues in tandem.

ANGEL CITY 4:
> Try to track her down,
> Go over the whole town.
> Better have hope and both eyes open
> Ev'rybody's gotta be somewhere.
>
> Girls don't vanish in thin air.
> She's lying low, you're flying blind, but

Ev'rybody's gotta be somewhere,
Ev'rybody's gotta be somewhere.
    (STONE *has no success finding* MALLORY)

*Scene 16*

**INT.    STONE'S PLACE — NIGHT**

> *Dark, shadowy. No one there, until* STONE *enters.*
> *As he hangs up his coat and hat and drapes his*
> *jacket and holstered gun on a chair:*

STONE'S VOICE (*Over*):    "The one advantage to living alone was you never had to lie to anyone about what a great day you'd had. Looking for Mallory Kingsley was about as refreshing as a quick dip in a cesspool. And just as rewarding. For now, it was time to hit the sack."
> *(After a sudden movement under the bed sheet:)*
> "Living in earthquake country, sometimes the sack hits you."
> *(He draws his gun, whips the sheet aside to reveal*
> *a naked, cheerful* MALLORY KINGSLEY)

STONE:    Hold it!

MALLORY:    Hi!

ANGEL CITY 4 (*Reappearing off to one side, sing*):
Everybody's gotta be somewhere!
> *(Blackout on* ANGEL CITY 4. *As* STONE *looks down*
> *at* MALLORY:)

STONE'S VOICE (*Over*):    "It was Mallory Kingsley. And for a missing girl, there was not a whole lot missing."

MALLORY: Surprised?

STONE: How'd you know it was my birthday?

MALLORY (*Sings*):
Mr. Detective, you've been looking too hard,
You should have started looking in your own back yard.
 (STONE *covers her with the sheet and turns on the*
 *lights*)
Lost and found,
Lost and found.
You've earned your salary,
Searching for Mallory.
Wanna play lost and found?
Well, then, here I am
On the lam.
You've been assigned to find out where I've been
And now you've found me in your bed.
And though my daddy said to turn me in,
Why don't I turn you on instead?

Teasing lips,
Pleasing thighs,
Easy on
Private eyes.

If you're not celibate,
We could raise hell a bit.
Why don't you call my bluff?
Don't resist,
You won't know what you've missed . . .
You'll never tame me,
But you can claim me
At the lost and found.
 (*Lights fade, as* MALLORY *starts to untie his tie*)

*Scene 17*

DONNA's *bedroom. Their lovemaking over,* DONNA *finishes tying* STINE's *tie.*

STINE:  Thank you.

DONNA:  I love men's ties. They're one more thing to hold on to.

STINE:  I noticed a few in the closet. Trophies?

DONNA:  Consolation prizes.
               (*Beat*)
You could spend the night.

STINE:  I've got to call New York.

DONNA:  My phone reaches there.

STINE:  I hate lying in front of an audience. I've got some work to do anyway.

DONNA:  You love your wife, you know that, don't you?

STINE:  I do.
               (*On reflection*)
Strange phrase in this context.

DONNA:  Then how do you explain being here?

STINE:  Hate doing my tie alone, I guess. Or at least without someone I care about.

DONNA: Right. What's your line? "Some guys'll crawl out of the grave to cheat?"

STINE: It's Oolie's.

DONNA: You wrote it.

STINE: I just put down what my characters tell me. I'm nowhere as smart as they are.
(*He is ready to go*)

DONNA: Which one of them's telling you to leave?

STINE: Stone.
(*Kisses her brow*)
He's got a streak of morality that somehow eludes me.
(*Lights fade, as we resume:*)

*Scene 18*

**RESUME STONE'S PLACE — NIGHT**

> MALLORY, *still in her bed sheet, is untying a reluctant* STONE'*s tie.*

STONE (*Stopping her*):  First, you level.

MALLORY:  Level?

STONE:  About why you're here. I don't remember you coming back with these sheets from the laundry.

MALLORY:  It's simple, Mr. Stone. I want half of whatever Daddy's paying you to find me. I've earned it, haven't I? How many other lost people have turned up in your bed?

STONE:  Until tonight, just me. And where exactly do I tell Daddy I found you?

MALLORY:  Tijuana, Frisco. He won't care. Just as long as baby's back.

STONE:  Then why does baby have to go through all this for what has to be petty cash in your family?

MALLORY:  Don't let Luther Kingsley's condition fool you, just 'cause he looks like a hot dog on a roll. He wants to know what the score is all the time. I can't tell him why I need the money.

STONE:  Blackmail?

MALLORY:   How did you guess?

STONE:   This is my room; I do very well here.

MALLORY:   I kind of had a thing with my tennis teacher last
year. A couple of other people, too. We all kind of had a
thing together. Sort of mixed doubles. Manuelo took
some pictures. I love how they came out, but I don't think
Daddy would.
>            (*Getting physical again*)
He thinks I'm a good girl. He just doesn't know *how*
good.

STONE (*Resisting her*):   So you got your stepmother to set up
the disappearance scam.

MALLORY:   Oh, no. Alaura thinks I really did run away. My
brother, Peter, and I worked it all out.

STONE:   And how come I got invited to the party?

MALLORY:   Peter's very thorough. He checked around, said
he found out you were real smart; that you knew how to
handle yourself. Do you *really* know how to handle yourself, Mr. Stone?
>            (*She forces him onto the bed, her body atop his.
>            With* STONE *at his most compromised, the door
>            flies open, a* MAN *steps into the room and takes a
>            flash picture of them, then disappears into the
>            night.* STONE *dashes out after him.* MALLORY *picks
>            up his revolver and runs out the open door and dis-
>            appears in the opposite direction.* STONE *returns to
>            find her gone, hears a car's tires squealing away
>            offstage, then discovers that his gun is gone, too. As
>            flashback effect begins:*)

STONE'S VOICE (*Over*): "Another dame. Another gun. Will I ever learn? Will I ever forget? Is my life going to be one, long flashback?"

## Scene 19

**INT.    THE CITY MORGUE — NIGHT**

*The Coroner,* HARLAN YAMATO, *wheels in the body of* IRWIN S. IRVING *on a gurney. Also present: Commissioner of Police* GAINES. *Speaking into the wall pay phone is* MAHONEY, *a studio press agent.*

MAHONEY:   Mahoney. City morgue. Take this down, babe. It goes out as the official studio release. "July 17, Hollywood, California. Movieland and filmgoers the world over mourn today the sudden passing in his sleep of industry pioneer and celluloid giant, Irwin S. Irving . . ."

YAMATO (*To* GAINES):   One bullet entered between the third and fourth ribs, then penetrated the thorax . . .

MAHONEY:   "Death came peacefully to the motion picture mogul and philanthropist extraordinaire . . ."

YAMATO:   The second bullet shattered the right kidney. All in all, an obvious heart attack.

MAHONEY:   Right.

(*He hangs up*)

YAMATO:   Commissioner?

GAINES (*Signing a document*):   I've seen pigs die better.

YAMATO:   Not when they go with their pants down.

87

GAINES (*Calls off*):   Stone.
>    (STONE, *minus the adhesive and wearing his po-
>    liceman's uniform, enters.* YAMATO *and* MAHONEY
>    *exit, as* GAINES *crosses to* STONE, *who surrenders
>    his police badge and his gun belt to him.* GAINES
>    *exits, leaving* STONE *alone. A beat, then* BOBBI,
>    *filled with guilt and remorse, appears*)

STONE (*To* BOBBI):   It's alright. No one'll ever know. It never
happened.

BOBBI:   Unless you were there when it didn't.
>                  (*Beat*)
> What now?

STONE:   There're other towns, babe. Other jobs.

BOBBI:   Other memories?
>    (*A rueful glance at* IRVING's *body on the gurney*)
> My chance to be somebody. Somebody I can't stand to
> be.

STONE:   Time, Bobbi. Give it time.

BOBBI:   That's one thing I've had enough of.
>    (*She gives him a kiss filled with longing and de-
>    spair; then, stepping back from him*)
> Forget me.

STONE:   The minute I die.
>    (BOBBI *exits. A beat, then* MUNOZ, *in his police-
>    man's uniform, enters behind* STONE)

MUNOZ:   You're getting away with it, you son-of-a-bitch.
Getting away with murder.

STONE:   I was ready to take my lumps.

MUNOZ: There're no God damn lumps for gringos. You want lumps? Be brown, be black, be yellow. Everything's smooth for you milky bastards. Kicked off the force. That don't even muss your hair. This happens to me, they hang me by my clockweights. Jesus, they'd fry me for jay-walking.

STONE: I didn't ask for this.

MUNOZ: You people don't have to ask. It comes with being in the club. Heads or tails, you always win, as long as the heads are blonde. First, you stole the land; now, you're murdering the law. The more you've got, the more there is to throw away, amigo. And you had it all. The badge. The right color skin.

STONE: You finished?

MUNOZ: Not till you are. Starting this minute, you're not going to need a scarf at night, not with my breath on your neck. I'm moving inside you. There's not one mirror you're not going to see me in. That better be the cleanest nose in town, 'cause I'll bust you for a bad haircut.
> (*Faces almost touching*)

Give me one more chance and I'll personally strap you into the gas chamber chair, sweetheart.

STONE: Maybe you could get 'em to put in a loveseat.
> (*He exits. A beat, then* MUNOZ *goes off. Only the gurney, with the body of* IRWIN S. IRVING *on it, remains on stage. Fade out*)

*Scene 20*

BUDDY *on a massage table that served as the gurney for* IRWIN S. IRVING *in the previous scene.* ANNA *is massaging him.* STINE *and* DONNA *are present.*

BUDDY (*Sitting up*): We agreed to not having that scene in the morgue, didn't we? Didn't we agree I was right, no Irwin S. Irving in the morgue scene?

STINE: Am I married to everything we agree to? I've been known to be creative on my own, you know. I mean, accidents *do* happen.

BUDDY: Does it say anywhere not to be creative? Did I dictate someplace, "Be a hack?" You can write whatever the hell comes into your head, I want you to, just so long as I like it in advance, and I'm telling you, that showing *two* morgue scenes is showing exactly one too many morgue scenes.
    (*Wincing, to* ANNA)
Ow! Jesus, take it easy! There's a person under this skin!
    (*Getting into a robe with* ANNA's *help; to* STINE)
Look, reading the book, I saw the whole movie from beginning to end. Frankly, it's a pain in the keester for me to have to shoot the God damn thing so everybody else can see it, but the studio can't sell tickets to my head, right? Just believe me. I've already seen this movie, and

that first morgue scene isn't in it, okay?

ANNA:   See you tomorrow, Mr. Fidler.
     *(She exits with the gurney,* BUDDY *giving her bottom a farewell pat)*

STINE:   But doing two morgue scenes let me establish Munoz's anger at Stone getting away with Irwin S. Irving's death.

BUDDY:   It'll be too confusing.

STINE:   Give the audience a little credit.

BUDDY:   Forget about credit. Movies is a cash business. They give us money, we make it easy for them.
               *(Beat)*
     Stine. Think, okay? Scene 27, Dr. Mandril at the edge of the mansion, overlooking the canyon, right?
               (MANDRIL *appears*)

MANDRIL (*Chants*):   Ommmm. . . .
               *(Arms outstretched, to someone offstage)*
     The power of prayer. You've come to me — as I knew one day you would, in all your loveliness.
               *(A woman's bare arm appears. Then, her other hand is seen, holding a revolver and firing one shot at the horrified* MANDRIL. *Lights fade on* MANDRIL, *as he dies)*

BUDDY (*To* STONE):   Okay. After he's murdered and they wheel him into the morgue, you can establish whatever you want about Munoz there.

STINE:   Fine, fine.
               *(Re pages)*
     Any other of this gold you find somewhat tarnished?

BUDDY:   I don't want to pick things to pieces.

STINE:   Pick.

BUDDY:   All that brown, yellow and black stuff with Munoz. Cut all that "my" people, "your" people, social crap. Just give me a good private eye show.

STINE:   It was the social *crap* that made the book more than just that.

BUDDY:   Stine, Stine. Guy's sitting in the movies, right? Fifty cents to get in. The balcony's comfy, all nice and dark. He's got his hand between somebody's legs next to him. It might even be somebody he knows. We all of a sudden gonna remind him that he's white and that the Pachuco usher might try to stab him in his throat on the way out? What made your book was how good you write. I'm not asking you to write bad.

STINE:   Just safe.

BUDDY:   You bet your ass! This town's crawling with congressmen. The last thing I need is for you to get blacklisted. You got any messages, put 'em in a letter. Then don't mail it. You got any idea how many close friends, how many personal relatives I can't have to my house for a bagel, just 'cause they mighta bought a Henry Wallace button at a rally?

STINE:   But how do I fuel Munoz? Without the racial angle, what makes him hate Stone so? Why his compulsion to see Stone punished?

BUDDY:   I don't care what it is, just change all that brown, black and yellow, to red, white and blue.

(*Beat*)

I know. Writing books is easier. But that way you don't get to see me naked, right?
> (*Opens his robe, flashes himself*)

STINE:   Sure wish I'd brought my magnifying glass.

BUDDY (*A "pained" expression*):   Oooooh.
> (*To* DONNA)

The boy is not happy.
> (*To* STINE)

Okay, okay, wait! I knew if you gave it enough thought, I'd come up with it. You ready? Munoz was *jealous of Stone*! He loved Bobbi, too. Almost went nuts when they got engaged. He *did* go nuts! It made him psycho! *That* gives him his heat! That gives Munoz his anger!

STINE:   That's garbage!

BUDDY:   Polish it! Make it shine! You like working in this town? You like having lunch ten feet from Betty Grable? Kill the politics. These guys from Washington aren't kidding around. They don't even want to get laid out here! Don't do anything to make the studio replace you.

STINE:   They'd only do that if you asked.

BUDDY:   Don't make me ask is what I'm asking. I can only protect you until I hafta start protecting myself. You wanna go down the toilet with your three-picture deal, I'm not going along for the ride sitting on your lap.

STINE:   Is that it for now?

BUDDY:   Donna, you got the list?

DONNA (*Reading from notes*):   "'Pretty girl with the clap.' 'Bang instead of a whimper.' 'Clockweights,' 'Milky bastards' — uh — 'God damn it' and 'Jesus'."

STINE:   Read the book.

BUDDY:   You can get away with all kinds of filth in a book, but this is motion pictures.

STINE:   Mustn't offend the guy in the balcony, right? He might lose his place in the person next to him?

BUDDY (*To* DONNA):   There was one more, wasn't there?

DONNA (*Checking her notes*):   Where Stone calls Irwin S. Irving a son-of-a-bitch.

BUDDY:   You know better. Don't use words you can't use. Don't cock up that scene. I know Irving's a shithead, so don't ask me why, but he's my favorite character in the show.
  (DONNA *laughs out loud.* BUDDY, *thinking she is*
  *laughing with him and not at him, laughs, too.*
  *Then, losing his smile, to* STINE:)
And just one morgue scene!

## *Scene 21*

**INT.   THE CITY MORGUE — NIGHT**

> YAMATO *wheels on the body of* DR. MANDRIL,
> MUNOZ *walking at his side.*

YAMATO:   There was no sign of a struggle. Dr. Mandril
went quietly into the night, the chief insult being this bullet, which entered his larynx, depriving the deceased of
both his voice and his life, probably in that order. Thirty-
eight caliber. From a service revolver, much like your
own. Any leads, Manny?

MUNOZ:   I got better than that.
> (*Covering* MANDRIL'*s face with a sheet*)
Pasco! Bring him in!
> (STONE *enters, prodded on by:*)

PASCO:   Lieutenant.

MUNOZ (*To* STONE):   Some guys order steak and potatoes for
their last meal. Pie à la mode's a big number. I'd start giving it some thought now, in case you want something
special.

STONE:   If you'd like to tell me what you're talking about,
maybe I'll know why I'm being bored.

MUNOZ:   Let me hear you on the subject of between seven
and nine tonight.

STONE:   I believe the answer to that is eight.

MUNOZ:   And you were where at the time?

STONE:   Home.

MUNOZ:   Whose?

STONE:   Mine.

MUNOZ:   Doing what?

STONE:   I don't remember you and me getting married.

MUNOZ:   You better play this one straight, pallie.
         (*He pulls the sheet back, to reveal* MANDRIL's *face.*
         STONE *is properly impressed*)

STONE:   I was there all night.

MUNOZ:   Can you prove it? Have any company?

STONE:   I was with someone.

MUNOZ:   You weren't alone.

STONE:   You've been going to crime school.

MUNOZ:   And just who were you not alone with?

STONE:   A young lady.

MUNOZ:   During those hours?

STONE:   We weren't watching the clock.

MUNOZ:   Will she back you up?

STONE:   I'm not sure.

MUNOZ:   Married?

STONE:   Missing.

MUNOZ:   Aw, that's a little bit of too bad, isn't it?
(*He snaps his fingers.* PASCO *hands him a photo*)
This wouldn't be her, would it? In bed with you, with her just a little south of the border?
(*To* PASCO)
Put the cuffs on him.
(*With a smile*)
Jackpot. Bingo, straight across. And I thought this was going to be a lousy day.
(*Sings*)
There's no sun up in the sky
And the birds forgot to sing,
But you're headed for a cell,
Then to die and rot in hell,
So it might as well be spring.
I'll be singing like a bird
When the jury sets the date.
And this capital event
Proves revenge is heaven sent.
All ya have to do is wait.

You're about to take that big siesta,
Stone, but don't request a
Padre rest a
— Ssured that I'll say mass.
Try a final meal of tacos on a
Plate of beans, mañana,
Odds are they are gonna
Give you gas.

They will strap you in a chair,
And for once you'll be polite.
You'll say, "Gov'nor, pardon me,"

But he's sure to disagree
'Cause the case I've made is tight.
It's the people versus Stone
And my money's on the state.
Who says dreams do not come true?
You will get what you are due.
All ya have to do is wait.

Time to fiesta.
On the day you die I'll eat high on the hog.
Santa Maria,
I will go to town on the day you're put down like a dog.
I'm leading an ovation
At your asphyxiation.

As crowds line up to watch you pay your debts,
I'll collect my bets,
Playing castanets.

As you're walking your last mile,
I'll be overcome with pride.
Taking pleasure in your death,
And to know your final breath
Will be filled with cyanide.
Though you've never been my fav'rite
Gringo,
In my native lingo.
Adios,
The end is close.
As they seal the chamber door
Think of me who sealed your fate.
Once the pellets hit the pail,
From the instant you inhale,
All ya have to do is wait.

Good things come to those who wait!

STONE (*Spoken*):   You got nothing on me.

MUNOZ:   Sebastian Mandril knew you and the Kingsley girl were playing footsies, way above the ankles, and he had the pictures to prove it. Afraid her old man'd find out, tired of being blackmailed, she begged you to get him off her back. Mandril goes through some kind of mumbo-jumbo meditation every night at the edge of the Kingsley estate, where it overlooks the canyon. You went there to try to pay him off, knock him off, finish it any way you could. There was a "discussion," the kind that always ends in a shot. If you hadn't panicked 'cause the staff came running, you'd've climbed down to get the pictures —
*(Producing* STONE's *revolver)*
and your gun. It took only one bullet. We found it in Mandril's voicebox. Even though he couldn't talk, it named you loud and clear.

STONE:   This is a frame.

MUNOZ:   Famous first words.

STONE:   Somebody set me up.

MUNOZ:   Whoever it is, I'm sending 'em roses.

STONE:   Listen to me. Last time was different, Manny.

MUNOZ:   Don't "Manny" me! Ever! The more you've got, the more there is to throw away, amigo.
*(Moving closer)*
And you had it all. The badge. The right color skin.
*(Lights up on* STINE, *as he appears, seated at his typewriter. He XXX's out what he has just written, causing* MUNOZ *to move to his previous*

*position and to recite his last line backwards.*
MUNOZ *and* STONE *freeze, until* STINE *inserts a*
*fresh sheet of paper and starts to type again:)*

MUNOZ (*Reactivated*):   And you had it all. The badge.
>                        (*Beat*)
Bobbi. Seeing what she saw in you, that was hard enough.
What killed me was the way she looked right through me
to see it.
>           (STONE *turns from* MUNOZ, *stares at* STINE *in*
>           *disbelief*)
The only thing that spoils your dying for me is the pain it
might cause her . . .

STONE (*To* STINE):   You really going to do this?
>                     (STINE *types, ignoring him*)

MUNOZ (*Unaware of the* STONE/STINE *exchange*):   If she's anywhere around to know about it.
>          (*He recedes into the shadows*)

STONE (*To* STINE):   You're going to cave in? Just like that?
>                     (*Beat*)
I wouldn't've believed it.

STINE:   You wouldn't've believed it? Is that what you said?
*You* wouldn't've believed it? You??
>                     (*Sings*)
You are some gumshoe,
You just don't think well.
Get this, dumb gumshoe,
You come from my inkwell.

Is your mouth lonely
With one foot in there?

Stone, your brain only
Holds thoughts I put in there.

Just what you are I'll spell out.
You are a novel pain,
One speck of lint that fell out
The last time that I picked my brain.

STONE:
    You are so jealous
    Of my track record.
    Tolstoy, do tell us
    Your feeble hack record.

    Your weak-knees brand you
    Soft and unstable.
    One small threat and you
    Fold like a card table.

    You drool at my adventures,
    Your broads in bed are bored.
    Go home and soak your dentures,
    Your pen is no match for my sword.

BOTH:
    You're nothin' without me.
    A no one who'd go undefined,
    You wouldn't exist,
    You'd never be missed.

STINE:
    I tell you you're out of *my* mind.

BOTH:
    A show off, a blowhard,
    You're equal parts hot air and gall

And no one would doubt me
Without me you're nothin' at all.

STINE:

You're in my plot
I'm still your creator.
I call each shot,
I'm your private dic-tator.

STONE:

You are so thick, you
Eat, breathe, sleep fiction.
I'm your meal ticket
Knee-deep in cheap fiction.

STINE:

You gloating ignoramus,
You haven't any shame.

STONE:

Hey, I'm a famous shamus
And most people don't know your name.

BOTH:

You're nothin' without me.
Without me you'd just disappear
Right into thin air,
And no one would care,
Or notice you ever were here.

A puppet, an upstart,
A loser who's destined to fall.
I'm everything you always wanted to be,
Let's deal with the issue:
You wish you were me.
You're nothin' without me.

Without me you're nothin' . . .
> (*To prove his dominance over* STONE, STINE *resumes typing, reactivating* MUNOZ, *who steps back into the light*)

MUNOZ (*Spoken, to* STONE):   Let's go!

STONE:   Manny, wait!

MUNOZ:   I said, keep my name out of your mouth!
> (MUNOZ *punches* STONE *hard, in the stomach, sending* STONE *to his knees.* STONE *stares at* STINE, *a character betrayed*)

STONE:   You bastard!
> (STINE, *ignoring him, types four letters*)

STINE:   "Fade . . ."
> (*Types three more letters*)

"Out."
> (*And the lights do just that, on* MUNOZ *and* STONE. *Then* STINE *sings, triumphantly:*)

You're nothin' without me,
Without me you're nothin' at all.
> (*Curtain*)

STONE (James Naughton)

OOLIE (Randy Graff)

ALAURA KINGSLEY (Dee Hoty)

STONE: " . . . and only the floor kept her legs from going on forever."

STONE (James Naughton) and ALAURA (Dee Hoty)

STINE (Gregg Edelman)

BIX SIX (Herschel Sparber), SONNY (Raymond Xifo) and
STONE (James Naughton)

"Ya Gotta Look Out for Yourself"

JIMMY POWERS (Scott Waara, *center*) and THE ANGEL CITY 4
(Gary Kahn, Jackie Presti, Amy Jane London, Peter Davis)

"What You Don't Know About Women"
GABBY (Kay McClelland) and OOLIE (Randy Graff)

"The Buddy System"
DONNA (Randy Graff) and BUDDY FIDLER (Rene Auberjonois)

"With Every Breath I Take"
BOBBI (Kay McClelland)

"The Tennis Song"
ALAURA (Dee Hoty) and STONE (James Naughton)

The Search
(Tom Galantich, James Naughton, Jacquey Maltby)

"Lost and Found"

MALLORY KINGSLEY (Rachel York) and STONE (James Naughton)

"All Ya Have to Do Is Wait"

MAHONEY (James Hindman) YAMATO (Alvin Lum), STONE
(James Naughton), OFFICER PASCO (Tom Galantich) and
MUNOZ (Shawn Elliott)

"You're Nothing Without Me"
STINE (Gregg Edelman) and STONE (James Naughton)

"Stay With Me"

JIMMY POWERS (Scott Waara, *center*) and THE ANGEL CITY 4
(Peter Davis, Jackie Presti, Gary Kahn, Amy Jane London)

CARLA (Dee Hoty) and BUDDY (Rene Auberjonois)

The garden of BUDDY's Bel-Air mansion (Rene Auberjonois, *center*)

STINE (Gregg Edelman)

AVRIL RAINES (Rachel York)

"It Needs Work"

GABBY (Kay McClelland) and STINE (Gregg Edelman)

STONE (James Naughton) and BOBBI (Kay McClelland)

The Finale

# ACT II

## *Scene 1*

*A recording studio.* JIMMY POWERS *and the* ANGEL
CITY 4.

JIMMY & ANGEL CITY 4 (*Sing*):
    I'm in a sentimental way,
    So stay with me.
    I'll ask the orchestra to play
    Your fav'rite song.
        (JIMMY *stops singing, to the annoyance of the*
        ANGEL CITY 4, *and clears his throat elaborately.*
        *Then, to* STUDIO ENGINEER:)

JIMMY:    Okay, Pops.

STUDIO ENGINEER:    Jimmy Powers. "Stay with Me." Take
    thirty-six.

JIMMY & ANGEL CITY 4 (*Sing*):
    I'm in a sentimental way,
    So stay with me.
    I'll ask the orchestra to play
    Your fav'rite song.

    Thoughts that we would blush to say
    Come easily in song,
    So why the rush to say so long?

    There's no one calling you away,

So stay with me.
What say we while away the day
And pay the price?
For just this once,
Let's not think twice.

These stolen moments that we spend
Never have to end.
Save them in your heart.
I know they're sure to stay with me
Even after we must part.

>   (*The quality of the sound of the music changes, as
>   lights fade on* JIMMY *and the* ANGEL CITY 4)

## Scene 2

*Music becomes tinnier, now heard on a phono-
graph in a Bel-Air bedroom. A woman, in a satin
robe, with matching lingerie, sits on the bed,
brushing her hair, enjoying the last few bars of the
record. When it's over, she starts it again, sits and
begins reading some screenplay pages. Appearing to
be* ALAURA KINGSLEY, *she is, in fact,* CARLA
HAYWOOD, BUDDY's *wife.* BUDDY, *in a mono-
grammed robe, enters, fresh from the shower, applying cologne and singing along with the record,
badly. Then:*

BUDDY (*Spoken*):   *Now* you're reading? People'll be here.
          (CARLA *goes on reading*)
    Mrs. Fidler, it's noon almost.

CARLA:   This script gets better and better.

BUDDY:   Gimme a clue. I'm only working on six at the moment.

CARLA:   "City of Angels."

BUDDY:   Better now, sure. You should see the pages *before* I
get 'em.

CARLA:   Buddy, I've got some thoughts about Alaura's first
scene. I think when she comes into Stone's office to hire
him, I should be dressed all in white.

133

BUDDY:   Save the suggestions, okay? I get enough of those from the writer. Sunday brunch, I'm not looking for a story conference. New earrings?

CARLA:   Mmm.

BUDDY:   You're not wearing 'em today?

CARLA:   *Now* I am.

BUDDY:   Wrong color for you. They're too big for your head.

CARLA:   Our problems are not dissimilar.

BUDDY:   You'll see, when somebody puts lox and cream cheese on 'em.

CARLA:   So somebody'll eat me, is that so terrible?

BUDDY (*Coming closer, grinning*):   Not so terrible at all.

CARLA:   Buddy . . . you just got out of the shower.

BUDDY:   I think I could find it again.
   (*Before joining her on the bed, to the phonograph:*)
Sing it, Jimmy, sing it.
   (*Music up, as lights fade*)

*Scene 3*

**INT.   A JAIL CELL — NIGHT**

> STONE's *visitor, clearly roused in the middle of the night, is* OOLIE, *a scarf on her head, a raincoat over her nightgown.*

OOLIE:   A hundred thousand dollars bail?! Where're you supposed to get that kind of money?

STONE:   You wouldn't like to sell your body a hundred thousand times, would you?

OOLIE:   How 'bout just once, to a big spender?
> *(She hands him a few packs of smokes)*

Who do you figure?

STONE:   Set me up? You're going to have to be my legs. Do some checking around.

OOLIE:   Starting with the Kingsleys.

STONE:   They're closer than Denmark, and a lot more rotten. Try the public library, back issues of the *Times*. Do some trolling. See who we know might know something they figure no one else does.

OOLIE:   I knew she was trouble. I only had to take one look. One look at you taking one look at her. She should've never got past me. I never learn.

STONE:  I don't seem to either.

OOLIE:  That's what it is I never learn.
    (*The* GUARD *appears. Time's up*)

GUARD:  Stone.

STONE:  Good girl, Oolie.
    (*As* STONE *joins the* GUARD:)

OOLIE (*To herself*):  Good girl, Oolie.
  (STONE *is lead off by the* GUARD. *As* OOLIE *begins to sing, lights up on:*)

*Scene 4*

INT.   **OOLIE'S BEDROOM — NIGHT**

> OOLIE *enters, hangs up her raincoat and scarf and gets into bed.*

OOLIE (*Sings*):
> I'm one of a long line of good girls
> Who choose the wrong guy to be sweet on;
> The girl with a face that says "welcome,"
> That men can wipe their feet on.
>
> I'm there when he calls me,
> The trusted girl Friday alright,
> But what good does it do me
> Alone on a Saturday night?
>
> If you need a gal
> To go without sal'ry and work too hard,
> You can always count on me.
> The kind of a pal
> Who'd sneak you a file past the prison guard,
> Loyal to the nth degree.
> The boss is quite the ladies man
> And that's my biggest gripe,
> Till I showed up he's never hired a girl 'cause she could type.
> I'm no femme fatale

But faithful and true as a Saint Bernard
Barking up the wrong damn tree,
You can always count on me.
> (*She winds up her alarm clock, then turns out the
> lamp on her bedside table. Music contines. In the
> dark, an alarm clock goes off. A lamp is turned on,
> revealing* OOLIE's *bedroom, now transformed
> into:*)

## Scene 5

DONNA's *bedroom.* STINE, *in pajamas, is in the
same bed just occupied by* OOLIE — *a woman
asleep at his side.* STINE *opens the blinds, waking
her. It is* DONNA.

STINE:   How long these things at Buddy's usually last?

DONNA:   Three, three-thirty, whichever comes first.

STINE:   I better shower. Shave, if I can bring myself to look
in the mirror.

DONNA:   You always wake up feeling guilty?

STINE:   I like to get an early start.

DONNA:   The change you made in the Munoz scene works.
It's fine.

STINE:   If you don't know what was there before. If you
don't know I caved in.

DONNA:   Collaborating is not caving in.

STINE:   Collaborating is working with the enemy.

DONNA:   You're too tough on yourself.

STINE:   There're some who're tougher.

DONNA:   You wake up with her, no matter who you go to
sleep with, don't you?

STINE: All she asks is that I be the best possible me. I keep settling for being a first draft.

DONNA: I don't have any problem with that.

STINE (*Exiting*): Don't make it easy. I need the pain.

DONNA: It's a big club.

(*Sings*)

I don't need a map,
I nat'rally head for the dead end street.
You can always count on me.
I'm caught in a trap;
When joy is approaching then I retreat.
I'm at home with misery.
I've been "the other woman" since my puberty began,
I crashed the junior prom
And met the only married man.
I'm always on tap
For romance or choc'late that's bitter sweet.
You can always count on me.

I go for the riff raff
Who's treating me so so;
When I can play the second fiddle
I'm a virtuoso.
I should be playing for a wedding band,
But there're no wedding rings attached,
Though you can bet there're strings attached.

A matter of fact,
If you want an ill-fated love affair,
You can always count on me.
Though I've made a pact
To carry out research before I care,

Men don't give a warranty.
One Joe who swore he's single
Got me sorta crocked, the beast;
I woke up only slightly shocked that I'd defrocked a priest.
Or else I attract
The guys who are longing to do my hair.
You can always count on me.

STINE (*Re-enters, dressing. Spoken*):   Wish you were going to be at Buddy's party.

DONNA:   It's just for the cast, nobody below the rank of colonel. If you've been to one, the rest are all remakes. "Baby!" "Sweetie!" "Loved your last picture!" "Crazy about your next!" They're better at brunch than they are on the screen. For best performance of a husband-in-the-dark, watch Buddy acting like he doesn't know.

STINE:   Doesn't know what?

DONNA:   About his wife and Jimmy Powers having the thing of the year. Which Buddy set up beautifully without either one of *them* knowing.

STINE:   Why would he do a thing like that?

DONNA:   Ah, with Buddy you have to wait till the last reel.

STINE:   Irwin S. Irving lives! Will you be here afterwards?

DONNA:   I've got some errands. I'll wait at your hotel. You've got more interesting cracks in your ceiling.
    (STINE *throws her his hotel key and exits. She sings*)
Though my kind of dame
No doubt will die out like the dinosaurs,
You can always count on me.

I'm solely to blame,
My head gives advice that my heart ignores.
I'm my only enemy.
I choose the guy who cannot introduce the girl he's with;
There're lots of smirking motel clerks who call me Mrs.
    Smith.
But I've made a name
With hotel detectives who break down doors.
Guess who they expect to see?
You can always count on,
Bet a large amount on,
You can always count on me.
                  (*Blackout*)

*Scene 6*

*A Bel-Air garden, reminiscent of the Kingsley mansion. A pianist is playing a reprise of "Double Talk," as* DEL DACOSTA *joins the* GUESTS.

BUDDY: Del! Del, baby! Everybody know Del DaCosta, Composer to the Stars?

DEL: Know me? I owe alimony to half these people! And some of the *women*, too!
(*As* DEL *and* GUESTS *mime chat:*)

BUDDY (*Sings, re* DEL):
This tin pan putz is not the pick of the litter;
There's not a clever note in his head.
But what's invaluable
Is he's so malleable,
And Steiner's at Warners
And Mozart and Gershwin are dead.

DEL (*Spoken*): What does anybody want to hear?
(*Replacing the pianist*)
Just name it and I can play it — just as long as I wrote it!

BUDDY: And he probably wrote it right after somebody played it! There's food over here, there's food over there. There's enough food to make you sick!
(BUDDY *continues soundlessly, as:*)

GUESTS (*Sing, re* BUDDY):
This pompous schmuck is making me nauseous,
Somebody ought to set him on fire.
I know where he can go
And I would tell him so,
Except that the day that I do is the day that I retire.
> (DEL *plays a snatch of "All You Have to Do Is Wait," as the actor who plays* MUNOZ, PANCHO VARGAS, *enters*)

PANCHO (*Spoken*):   Buddy!

BUDDY:   Pancho Vargas!

PANCHO (*Hugging him*):   Thanks for the Munoz part! I love him!

BUDDY:   Nada, baby, nada!
> (*To* GUESTS, *re* PANCHO)

Am I wrong? This guy never gets old. He's gotta be drinking monkey glands, right?
> (PANCHO *laughs a hearty employee's laugh, as* BUDDY's *study appears,* STINE *using the phone*)

*Scene* 7

BUDDY's *study*.

STINE: The usual crowd. The traveling compliment show. Everyone thrilled with everyone's success; positively orgasmic at anyone's failure. Envy so thick, you can cut it with the knife lodged in every other back. The script's going along pretty well. Some interesting changes I sort of like. At any rate, Buddy does, therefore, I do.
*(Listens; then, concerned)*
You called the hotel? . . . My hotel? When? . . . Five minutes ago? Look, hold on, will you? I can explain. She was there to —
*(Beat)*
Gabby? Gab?
*(Lights fade on a troubled* STINE*)*

### Scene 8

**INT.   THE JAIL — NIGHT**

MUNOZ *is handing* STONE *his personal belongings.*

MUNOZ (*Grudgingly*):   You know how to murder the right people, I'll give you that.

STONE:   Who put up the bail?

MUNOZ:   Like you don't know, huh?

STONE:   No one with a hundred thousand big ones that would help me.

MUNOZ:   Somebody rich with no taste is my guess.
(*In returning* STONE's *key chain,* MUNOZ *deliberately drops it on the floor so that* STONE *has to bend down to retrieve it. When* STONE *starts to go:*)
Stone.
(*He hands him a clipboard to sign a release form*)
Don't leave town. You're still my number one suspect.

STONE (*Signing*):   You're aces with me, too.
(*He deliberately drops the clipboard on the floor, infuriating* MUNOZ, *and walks off*)

## Scene 9

BUDDY's *study.* STINE *is still on the phone.*

STINE: Someone *has* to answer, Operator. I was just talking to the party; I know they're there. I mean, they couldn't just —
(*Resigned*)
Never mind. Fine. Thank you.
(*As he hangs up,* AVRIL RAINES, *a starlet, appears. She is played by the same actress we've seen as* MALLORY)

AVRIL: You suppose Mr. Fidler's read all these books?

STINE: Wrote most of them, too. Or will.
(*Offstage,* DEL *plays "Lost and Found"*)

AVRIL: You're Mr. Fidler's writer.

STINE: Found me in a basket on his doorstep.

AVRIL: I'm not interrupting, am I? I read somewhere that writers are always thinking. Even when they don't want to.

STINE: We live for the interruptions.

AVRIL: I'm Avril Raines.

STINE: I don't think I've ever seen a better one.

AVRIL: Avril's French for April.

STINE: Oui, je sais.

AVRIL: The only French I really know is my name.
(*Beat*)
I'm going to play Mallory Kingsley in the movie.

STINE: Why doesn't that surprise me?

AVRIL: I read every word of the book. From cover to cover.

STINE: It tends to make more sense that way.

AVRIL: I was so shocked when Mallory gets killed, I started crying. And I was all alone in bed, can you believe that? I mean, she was only what, at the most? Twenty-one?

STINE: Ah, well, the good die young. The naughty, even younger.

AVRIL: Mr. Fidler said it was going to be different in the movie. He said Mallory was going to be in it right up to the end.

STINE: I'm afraid Mr. Fidler's wrong.

AVRIL: How can he be? He's the producer-director. It's *his* movie.

STINE: His movie, *my* script.

AVRIL: I'd do anything for Mallory not to die, Mr. Stine.
(*Turning it on*)
I mean, anything you could possibly think of.
(*She moves from* STINE, *as* CARLA *enters, a drink in hand*)

CARLA: Mr. Stine. I'm Carla Haywood. Buddy's wife. And please don't tell him I gave him second billing.
(*Handing* STINE *the glass*)

Scotch and soda, wasn't it?

STINE:   Thank you.

CARLA:   There's tons of food out there, Avril.

AVRIL:   I was talking to Mr. Stine.

CARLA:   And now it's time to be hungry, dear.

AVRIL (*Exiting*):   You won't forget, Mr. Stine? Please?

CARLA (*To* STINE):   What do you think of your Mallory?

STINE:   Young and ripe.

CARLA:   "She'll get over it. We're all that for about thirty seconds."

STINE:   No author ever got angry being quoted to himself.

CARLA (*Striking an* ALAURA *pose*):   And what do you think of your Alaura Kingsley?

STINE:   I never thought of her as anyone else.

CARLA:   Wouldn't do you any good if you did. It's hard to replace someone who's sleeping with the director. Of course, in this director's case, that's a cottage industry. I've been peeking at the pages as you finish them.

STINE:   Then we're both up to the same place.

CARLA:   I'm not one to pat myself on the back, but I guessed who put up the bail for Stone when I read the book.

STINE:   Most people think it was one of the Kingsleys. They're the only ones I established with that kind of money.

CARLA:   I knew you wouldn't be that obvious.

149

STINE:  Never intentionally.
>(*Lights up on a dingy shed, filled with oil drums.* BIG SIX *is tying a trussed-up* STONE *to an overhead rail, while* SONNY *wires a complicated device to the phone.* DEL, *offstage, plays "Ya Gotta Look Out for Yourself"*)

STONE (*To* BIG SIX):  That's pretty good for a guy probably can't tie his own shoes.

CARLA (*To* STINE):  May I be perfectly honest?

STINE:  Can honesty be *im*perfect?

BIG SIX (*To* STONE):  Watch your mouth while you still got one.

CARLA:  Making the two hoods Mandril followers seemed awfully contrived. They were just too, I don't know, "hoody," I guess, to be that.

STINE:  I've changed it; given them another motivation.

STONE (*To* BIG SIX):  How do *you* mugs figure in all this?

BIG SIX:  Dr. Mandril, he took out a kinda insurance policy with us. He figured not being too popular with some people, if anybody ever shortened his life, we was to turn around and do exactly likewise. This is what you might call a pre-paid hit, right, Sonny?

CARLA (*To* STINE):  That's better. I like that.

STONE (*To* BIG SIX):  He wanted to prove there was death after life, did he?

BIG SIX:  Right.
>(*Taping* STONE's *mouth*)

His *and* yours. Ya finished, Son?

SONNY (*Turning the device on*):   Here we go.
(*A ticking is heard.* SONNY *explains to* STONE)
First time the phone rings, the cap gets snapped. Second ring, the fuse is exposed. The third ring ignites it an' then you an' this warehouse are somewhere over the Rockies.

BIG SIX:   How 'bout we go to the corner and make a call?

SONNY:   Good idea. Mr. Stone'd prolly like to get one, bein' here all on his own an' all.

BIG SIX:   So long, Mr. Stone.

SONNY:   Have a nice flight.
(*They exit. The ticking stops*)

CARLA (*To* STONE, *hooked*):   They leave him all alone?

STINE:   With just the ticking.
(*The ticking starts again, only louder, as* STONE's *mind races: "How to get out of this?" Suddenly, the phone rings. The ticking gets louder.* STONE *struggles, finally frees his hands from the overhead rail. The phone rings a second time. The ticking gets even louder.* STONE *turns on a nearby buzzsaw and cuts through the ropes that still bind his wrists. Before the phone can ring a third time,* STONE *scoops up the receiver*)

STONE (*Into phone*):   Sorry, I'm just on my way out!
(*Letting the receiver dangle, he exits, his feet still bound. Blackout on the shed*)

CARLA (*To* STINE):   I love it!

STINE:   Wait. There's a capper.

> (*Lights up on the shed again.* BIG SIX *and* SONNY
> *rush on, their guns drawn.* SONNY *picks up the
> frayed rope, stops the whirling buzzsaw*)

SONNY:   So that's how he got the phone!

BIG SIX:   Right.
> (*He puts the receiver back on the cradle. The phone
> rings immediately. Puzzled*)
Who knows to call us here?
> (*There is a blinding explosion and the dingy room
> is gone*)

CARLA (*Applauding, to* STINE):   Wonderful!

STINE:   Thank you.

CARLA:   Stone's next stop is Alaura's?

STINE (*Nods*):   Next stop, Alaura's.
> (*Offstage,* DEL *plays "Stay with Me," followed by
> laughter and applause, as* JIMMY POWERS *is heard
> singing the lyrics*)

CARLA (*Brightening*):   Please excuse me!
> (*She makes a hasty exit*)

## Scene 10

BUDDY's *garden.* DEL *accompanies* JIMMY POWERS.
GUESTS *listen appreciatively, none more so than*
CARLA, JIMMY *addressing the lyrics to her.*

JIMMY (*Sings*):
I'm in a sentimental way,
So stay with me.

ANGEL CITY 4:
Stay with me.

JIMMY:
I'll ask the orchestra to play
Your favorite song.

ANGEL CITY 4:
They're gonna play your favorite song.

BUDDY (*Spoken, interrupting*):   Beautiful! Beautiful!
(*Re* DEL)
And *then* he wrote!
(DEL *begins another tune.* CARLA *walks* JIMMY
*away, unaware that* BUDDY *has his eye on them*)

JIMMY (*Conspiratorially*):   I love your earrings.

CARLA (*Coyly*):   Thank you.

JIMMY:   Did he ask where you got them?

CARLA:   I took his mind off the question.
        (*To* STINE, *who is surrounded by* AVRIL)
Here's the perfect meeting of words and music. Mr. Stine, Jimmy Powers.

JIMMY:   I'm a fan, sir. You're a master wordsmith.

AVRIL:   Isn't he ever just?

CARLA (*A smile that's an order*):   Time for seconds, dear.
        (AVRIL *walks off with her full plate. To* STINE *and* JIMMY)
I'll get you boys some goodies. Don't move.
        (*As* CARLA *leaves them:*)

BUDDY (*Calls out*):   Stine! You gotta hear this!

STINE (*To* JIMMY):   Tell her I moved.
        (*He crosses to* BUDDY)

BUDDY (*To* DEL):   Play it for him.
        (*To* STINE)
Listen to this melody. You'll think your ears are getting laid.

DEL:   It's not finished. I haven't written the release.

BUDDY:   I told you how it should go. You know.
        (*He sings the opening bars of "Tara's Theme" from "Gone With the Wind." The* GUESTS *join in*)

DEL:   I know. I love it. I'm just not sure it works.

BUDDY:   You gonna quetion me about music? You know how much I gave the Symphony last year?

DEL:   Wait, okay? Wait?

(*As* DEL *noodles experimentally:*)

BUDDY (*Aside, to* STINE *re* JIMMY):    They're false. Tops and bottoms.

STINE:    What's that?

BUDDY:    His teeth.

(*Sneers*)

America's favorite balladeer. America should see his mouth go to sleep in a glass every night. Still, the guy is never outta the Hit Parade; his records don't sit in the stores a minute. Go figure, huh?

(*To* DEL, *still working on a combination of three or four notes*)

Del! There's eighty keys! Try a few others!

DEL:    I think I've got it.

BUDDY:    Was I right?

DEL:    Mostly, yeah.

BUDDY:    Mostly is often enough.

(*To* STINE)

You ready? This is "Alaura's Theme." Picture it under the bedroom scene. Carla wearing satin, maybe less. Ten thousand violins. There won't be a dry seat in the house!

(DEL *starts "Alaura's Theme," his piano version giving way to a lush orchestral and choral rendition, as we enter:*)

*Scene 11*

INT.    ALAURA KINGSLEY'S BEDROOM — NIGHT

> ALAURA, *in a satin nightgown, sits on the bed, brushing her hair. A sudden shattering of glass, and a tense and dangerous* STONE *enters through the window, gun in hand.*

ALAURA (*Alarmed*):   Stone!

STONE (*His hand over her mouth*):   Let me tell you something about a hundred bucks, Mrs. Kingsley. A hundred bucks can buy a whole lot in this marked-down world. What it *can't* buy is anybody threatening to lift my shield if I don't take a case I normally wouldn't handle with ice tongs. And it for sure doesn't buy framing rights for a murder, or my being sprung by two gorillas, hot to make me a stiff for killing a man I barely laid eyes on, let alone ever a glove. What's it all about, Mrs. Kingsley? And let's have the truth, first time around.

ALAURA:   It's Peter, my stepson. He's got only one goal in life. To inherit Luther's money when he dies.

STONE:   He'd get his share, wouldn't he?

ALAURA:   He wants it all. Every bit of it. Peter saw Mandril getting more and more control over my husband. He and Mallory cooked up the scheme about her disappearing. It was Peter who took the pictures of you, who had Mallory steal your gun when you were together, to leave at the scene of the murder.

STONE: You knew the whole plan?

ALAURA: Peter boasted about it later. When I came to see you, I honestly thought she was missing. Just as I believe she is now. Or worse.

STONE: You saying he's finished her off, too?

ALAURA: If he hasn't, he will. And after Mallory, I'm the only one in the world who stands between him and the money. I'm frightened, Stone. So frightened.

STONE: Where is he now?

ALAURA: I don't know.
                    (*He grabs her, forcefully*)
I don't!
                    (*Beat, breathlessly*)
Without even touching, I felt this close the first time we met. Tell me you didn't know it, too.

STONE: You've got a way of feeling close even when you're not there.
                    (*She kisses him hard. On the break:*)
Why me? Of all the poor suckers who could've taken the rap, why me?

ALAURA: Only Peter can tell you. Find him and you'll know.

STONE: Got any idea which part of the haystack?

ALAURA: There's a place he goes. One place more than any other. I'll tell you where. Just promise me you'll do one thing when you find him.
                    (*Her hand to his gun*)

Shoot first!
    (*As they fall to the bed in an embrace: Blackout*)

*Scene 12*

BUDDY's *office.* BUDDY *sits at his desk. One of his phones is ringing.*

BUDDY (*Answering it*):   You got him? . . . Put him on.
      (*He hangs up receiver, picks up another*)
Stine? Donna tells me something you gotta tell me she's wrong. You're going to New York to see your wife? . . . Look, babe, this is something you ask, you don't tell, because I guarantee you, if you did, I would tell you you got no business asking. Writers don't go away when they're working. You don't leave in the middle of a movie . . . Never mind it's a weekend! Why can't she fly here? What do you have to knock yourself out flying back and forth, being here, being there, being here? There's too much to do yet. Sweetheart, you gotta put your personal life in the back seat in this business. You think I like being chained to this desk twenty-four hours a minute, seeing my own wife once every blue moon?
      (*Listens, then, angrily*)
Stine! I'm warning you in one word: don't leave town. You make me unhappy, you're going to find out I can return the compliment!
      (*A beat*)
Stine? Stine?!
      (*Hangs up violently*)
God damn it!

       *(He strikes his desktop with his riding crop)*
  Writers!
       *(A startled* AVRIL *appears from under his desk)*

AVRIL:  What was that?!
         *(Blackout)*

## Scene 13

STINE's *New York apartment.* GABBY *and* STINE;
*a chill in the room.*

STINE: We talk to each other only if we're both in the same
town, is that how it works from now on?

GABBY: I wouldn't count on it.

STINE: Long distance is a lot cheaper than airplane tickets
to New York.

GABBY: All depends on how much you want to spend on silence, I guess.

STINE: Can we talk about my letter?

GABBY: Your letter?

STINE: What'd you think?

GABBY: My professional opinion?

STINE: Gabby, we're not talking about fiction now.

GABBY: You could have fooled me.
(*Fetching the letter*)
God knows you're fooling yourself. You think making
Stone a hero allows you to act like anything *but* one. If
you want to write Hollywood endings, what about one for
us, where you start acting like he does, and he writes like
you do.

161

(*She takes a letter from a previously opened envelope and reads*)
"Okay, don't take my calls. If you won't listen, then read. One: Donna was obviously in my hotel room on Sunday when you phoned. Two: just remember no matter how incensed you were by 'One,' I was not there with her. Three: let me explain."
(*Aside*)
I do love an apology by the numbers.

STINE:   It's not an apology, it's an explanation.

GABBY (*Reading, overlapping his protest*):   "Trying to finish a new scene in time to bring to Buddy's brunch, naturally my typewriter picked that moment to start acting like a portable prima donna. An 'ortable rima donna,' actually, since the 'p' was just one of several keys that had decided to join the staff of the dead letter office. Half way out of the lobby, I bumped into Donna, half way in, having been dispatched by Buddy to make sure the pages got done, otherwise she could not have gotten into my room, where, using her own, far more reliable Corona to type up my notes, which she was doing when you called, while I was on my way to Buddy's, never dreaming that her presence, despite my absence, was going to cause you such needless, so easily-avoided pain."
(*End of letter*)
That's it? That's the explanation?

STINE:   That's it.

GABBY (*Sings*):
No lack of alibis
Your knack for the spectacular is still intact.
I like the tone of it;

It rings sincere and pretty near succeeds.
It's just the narrative
Is like a sieve and cloudy as a cataract.
There's not a trace of honesty, so face the fact:
It needs . . . work.

You dodge emotion, dear.
Your logic's unconvincing as it strains to please.
Unlike the books you write,
This plot is quite contrived the way it reads.
It's far too obvious;
And filled with flaws and gross implausibilities.
Excepting for the part about the broken keys
It needs work.

Your fiction always had
A little grit in it,
A little heart in it,
A little wit in it.
It used to be so clear
That there was art in it,
If you had written it,
So must you go and spit in it?

And come to think of it,
Your writing always mirrors our relationship,
With dangers cropping up
And sweet young strangers popping up like weeds.
So if you wish official pardoning,
You better do a little gardening,
Ya know ya needn't be so gen'rous with your seeds.
Your fertile lies don't fertilize;
It needs work.

We used to sit in bed and read each draft out loud.
We'd play each part and talk the story through.
Remember all we said and how we laughed out loud?
Now, take a closer look at you.
I oughta throw the book at you.

You had to ruin it.
This plot has got a a lot of déjà vu in it.
Familiarity —
And in this case we both know what that breeds.
But call me anytime you seem yourself,
When you've decided to redeem yourself,
When you discover where this self-deception leads.
I'd rather see you shoot yourself
Than watch you prostitute yourself,
Your new routine is too routine,
It needs work.

> (*By the finish, she has handed him his hat. Suit-case in hand,* STINE *exits, leaving a sad* GABBY *alone*)

## Scene 14

**INT.    MARGIE'S PLACE — THE PARLOR — NIGHT**

*One of* MARGIE's GIRLS *steps through the beaded curtains of an archway, wearing lingerie and a wrap. She stretches langorously.* STONE *enters, approaches her.*

GIRL (*Temptingly*):   Hi.
(MARGIE, *who appears behind her smoking a cigar, yanks the* GIRL *aside*)

MARGIE (*To* STONE):   Can I help you? Or are you just window shoppin'?

STONE:   I'm told there's a Peter Kingsley. One of your regulars.

MARGIE:   Peter Kingsley? Don't ring any bells.

STONE:   Six-one, about 24.

MARGIE:   He could be two-four, about 61. You stop noticin' after awhile.
(*Looking him over, appreciatively*)
Almost.

STONE:   He looks like money.
(*Offering her a bill*)
Tan, clean through.

MARGIE (*Taking the bill*):   Ah, I bet I know who you mean. Yeah. He's got a favorite here. She's the only one he ever asks for.

STONE:   Can I see her?

MARGIE:   It'll be expensive.

STONE:   I just want to talk.

MARGIE:   That's not cheap here either.
        (*Takes another bill from him and calls out*)
Bootsie!
        (BOOTSIE, *another of her girls, appears*)
Take this here gentleman here to the Red Room.
        (*To* STONE)
I'll send her in.
        (*As* BOOTSIE *leads* STONE *through the beaded curtain:*)
Have a nice chat.
        (*She laughs a raucous laugh. Lights fade on her, up on:*)

*Scene 15*

**INT.   THE RED ROOM — NIGHT**

*The first* GIRL *is sitting on the bed, painting her toenails, when* STONE *is ushered in by* BOOTSIE. *Both whores leave.* STONE *is alone a moment, then, behind his back, a woman enters, wearing something appropriate to her trade. It is* BOBBI.

BOBBI (*Pouring herself a whiskey*):   Would you like a drink?
    (STONE's *body stiffens at the sound of her voice*)
Rather not talk?

STONE (*Turning to her*):   Nothing you'd want to hear, Bobbi.

BOBBI (*Turning to face him*):   Why did I know this would happen sooner or later?

STONE:   Haven't I always been the answer to all your bad dreams?

BOBBI:   How'd you find me?

STONE:   The easiest way. By not looking.

BOBBI:   I never figured you for a place like this.

STONE:   Still able to read my mind.

BOBBI (*At the door*):   I'll get you someone else.

STONE:   Stay. You're paid for.

BOBBI (*Properly stung*):  Beatings cost extra.

STONE:  Tell me about Peter.

BOBBI:  I know a few.

STONE:  Try Kingsley.

BOBBI:  Peter Kingsley?

STONE:  You know a lot of those?

BOBBI:  What makes you think I know him at all?

STONE (*Putting his hat on the bed*):  Mostly the way you're pretending you don't.

BOBBI:  Is he in trouble?

STONE:  If I've got anything to say about it.

BOBBI:  He's not a bad guy.

STONE:  You would know. He's here a lot.

BOBBI:  More like sometimes.

STONE:  Like his car could drive here by itself? That kind of sometimes?
(*Looking around*)
Not exactly the movies, is it?

BOBBI:  We get to do our share of acting.

STONE:  With him, too? With Kingsley? Who do you play, little girl lost? "Let me take you away from all this," is that the routine? "What's a nice kid like you, et cetera?"
(*Beat*)
What *is* a nice kid like you, et cetera?

BOBBI: There was no way back for us. After. There was no way forward for me.

STONE: Does he know about us?

BOBBI: Who?

STONE: If this was a screen test, you'd flunk it.

BOBBI: I thought finally talking about it would help make it go away. It only keeps it alive.

STONE: You told Kingsley? Everything?
(*Reminding her*)
We had a deal.

BOBBI: I didn't say *I* pulled the trigger. I told him the official version. I passed out when you broke into the dressing room. When I came to, you were standing over Irving's body, your gun in your hand. As though repeating a lie over and over somehow makes it the truth.
(*Beat*)
I could have stayed, if you hadn't forgiven me. It was too much, having you take all the punishment.

STONE: Looks to me like we're about even.
(*Beat*)
Bobbi . . .

BOBBI (*Avoiding his touch*): Please . . .

STONE (*Sings*):
I try to tell myself
To let the memory of you die slow.
By letting time be my friend,
By letting go of what was,
The pain would end.
It never does.

BOBBI:

At any time or place,

STONE:

At anytime or place,
I close my eyes
And see
Your face
And
I'm embrac-
Ing you.

I close my eyes and
See your face

And I'm embracing you.
If only I believed

If
On-ly
I be-
Lieved that
Dreams
Come
True.

That
Dreams
Come true.

Dar-

At
Night out loud I pray:

Ling,
You were the one who said
Forever from the
Start,
And I've been drifting
Since you've gone.

Bobbi, go away.

How much must I take

Out on a lonely sea that only
You can chart,
I've been going on, knowing
That my
Heart
Will
Break

To end this ache?

I
Wel-
Come
Death
With each and ev'ry breath

With ev-'ry
Breath                              I
I
Take.                               Take.
   (STONE *recovers his hat and leaves.* BOBBI *is alone*
   *with her sorrow*)

*Scene 16*

**EXT.   A PUBLIC PHONE BOOTH — NIGHT**

OOLIE *is on the phone.*

OOLIE (*Into receiver*):   Drexel. West Virginia. Drexel.

STONE'S VOICE (*Offstage, filtered*):   Spelled the way it sounds? D-R-E- —?

OOLIE (*Cuts in*):   X-E-L. Right. Drexel.

STONE'S VOICE (*Offstage, filtered*):   Got it. And you managed to reach Peter Kingsley?

OOLIE:   He should be on his way.

STONE'S VOICE (*Offstage, filtered*):   Have I ever told you that I love you?

OOLIE:   Too many times to mean it. Be careful.
   (*A click at the other end, then a dial tone. He has hung up on her again. Then, to no one:*)
Be careful.
   (*Lights fade. Thunder and lightning deliver us to:*)

## Scene 17

**INT.    THE KINGSLEY SOLARIUM — NIGHT**

*Lightning and thunder, a wild wind punctuate the scene, as* ALAURA *lovingly spoon-feeds* LUTHER *inside his iron lung.*

ALAURA:  Slowly, darling. Measured breaths. Measured breaths. Let me wipe that tear. We all miss poor Dr. Mandril, don't we?
     (*Unannounced,* STONE *suddenly enters*)
Good evening, Mr. Stone. My husband's just having his dinner.

STONE:  The condemned man slurped a hearty meal? It'd make a lovely picture. Considering his chances with you around, you'd have to use very fast film.

ALAURA (*To* LUTHER):  Mr. Stone is a rather desperate man, darling. All sorts of people are after him; he's even wanted for murder.

STONE:  Which explains the look in these wild, bloodshot private eyes?
     (*Beat*)
The name William Lloyd Drexel ring a bell, Mr. Kingsley? West Virginia family. Mr. Drexel was in coal. Not personally, of course. A whole lot of strong, dirty men brought it up out of the ground for him.

ALAURA (*Continuing to feed* LUTHER, *coolly*):  Open wider, darling.

STONE:  Like you, Mr. Drexel had one foot, maybe a foot and a half in the grave, especially after *Mrs.* Drexel promoted herself from his private nurse to his future widow. Before he was shoveled into the same ground all his millions were shoveled out of, Mr. Drexel's children threw him a little going away autopsy. After they found traces of a long, toxic build-up in the smorgasbord that used to be their father, they threatened murder charges, forcing their grieving stepmother to give up her share of the inheritance.

(*To* ALAURA)

You weren't going to make the same mistake as Mrs. Kingsley you did as Mrs. Drexel, were you?

ALAURA (*Evenly*):  Not if I could help it, Mr. Stone.

STONE (*To* LUTHER):  This time she was going to make sure there'd be no other survivors. Only before she got rid of Peter and Mallory, there was the matter of Dr. Mandril, who was beginning to pray a lot more for your wealth than for your health and was getting more and more anxious to cash in on some of the looks your wife had been giving him that were hot enough to melt your tires.

(*To* ALAURA)

How'm I doing so far?

ALAURA:  Very good, Mr. Stone. Very good indeed.

STONE:  She arranged for your son, Peter, to kill Mandril and set me up as the fall guy, knowing that the police would readily accept me as a murder suspect.

(*To* ALAURA)

How were you going to do it?
            (*Re iron lung*)
Were you going to arrange for this to have a head-on collision with a streetcar? Or were you just going to pull the plug on your married appliance here?

ALAURA:  No, Mr. Stone.
            (*Producing a gun*)
*You* unhooked the machine; then you came at me. If I hadn't lost time shooting you in self-defense, I might have been able to get it started again.
            (*More thunder, more lightning*)

STONE:  And my motive?

ALAURA:  You knew that when my husband learned you'd murdered Dr. Mandril *and* that you were having an affair with Mallory, he'd have used his influence to put you in the gas chamber — for a whole week running. Isn't that true, Luther?
            (LUTHER *can only gasp pathetically. Calmly, reminding him*)
Measured breaths, darling, measured breaths.

STONE:  You're going to kill him before Peter and Mallory are safely out of the way?

ALAURA:  By now, Peter will have killed Mallory and be heading to the beach house to meet me. You've never seen it, Mr. Stone. Quite grand; it's on both sides of the highway. A private tunnel takes you to the water. "The old swimmin' hole," as my husband calls the Pacific. The house lies at the bottom of Kingsley Canyon, the road built to twist and twist, so that you can unwind on the way down, but not too much so — each side drops off

sharply a few hundred feet. When Peter's brakes — or what he *thinks* are his brakes — give out, he'll never make it past the first turn.
> (*Checking her watch*)

Which would have been just minutes ago.
> (*Gesturing at the iron lung's electric cord with her
> gun*)

And now, Mr. Stone, if you'll turn him off, I believe it's time my husband turned in. One swift pull should do it.

STONE:  You don't want the honor?

ALAURA:  I'll forego the pleasure for your fingerprints. I know you must think harshly of me, Luther, but that feeling won't last long.

LUTHER:  Alaura!!

ALAURA:  Night, night, darling.
> (STONE *doesn't move*)

*Now*, Mr. Stone!

LUTHER (*Whimpers*):  No, no. Stone, please, Stone.
> (PETER KINGSLEY *suddenly bursts through the
> doors*)

ALAURA:  Peter!
> (*Pointing at* STONE)

He was trying to kill Luther!

PETER (*Sneers*):  The same way he killed Mandril?

STONE:  I wasn't the only one set up, was I, kid?

PETER:  She did it! I didn't have the courage, thank God!

ALAURA:  I do love a coward with pride.

PETER: Anymore than I could do what she had in mind for Mallory!
(*A frightened* MALLORY *enters breathlessly, runs to* PETER's *side. To* STONE)
Did you know what Alaura had in mind for my father when you had your secretary tell me to meet you here?

STONE: I knew if we all met in one place, someone's tongue might come off its roller.
(*Turning to* ALAURA)
Now, about disconnecting Mr. Kingsley . . .

MALLORY: She wasn't!

ALAURA (*To* STONE): We can do it together! The two of us!
(*Re* PETER *and* MALLORY)
And then them! You don't know how much there is! We deserve it all! We've both gotten rotten deals out of life! Peter only had to tell me about you and that singer for me to know you took the blame for her.

STONE: Believe what you want. Your past and mine don't add up to the same future.

ALAURA (*Re gun*): Don't make me use this.

STONE (*Moving toward her*): That's the last thing I had in mind.

PETER: Stone!

MALLORY: Don't!
(STONE *puts his hand on* ALAURA's *gun.* ALAURA *does not let go. His body is close to hers, the weapon pressed between them. Three gun shots ring out.* MALLORY *screams*)

STONE'S VOICE (*Over*): "Three gunshots rang out."

> (STONE *falls to the floor*)

"Three shots, divided by two people . . ."

> (ALAURA, *still holding the gun, watches* STONE *fall, a look of victory on her face*)

"Somebody figures to die."

> (*A red stain appears beneath* ALAURA's *heart. It is blood. She falls to the floor, dead. As* STONE, *wounded, reaches to* PETER, *who kneels to help him:*)

"You can count it one of your better days if that someone doesn't turn out to be you."

> (*Iris out*)

*Scene 18*

STINE's *office.* DONNA *listens, as* STINE *reads from a script, his suitcase and hat parked beside his desk.*

STINE (*Disapprovingly*):  "You can count it one of your better days if that someone doesn't turn out to be you."
(*Turning to her*)
Where is he?

DONNA:   On the set. Production meeting.
(STINE *finds the copy of his novel on the desk. As he looks for a certain page:*)

STINE:   So much to do before he shoots a movie. Re-designing all the set designer's sets, personally biting off all the loose threads on the costumes, inventing the camera. It must kill him when a picture opens and someone else gets to butter the popcorn.
(*Finds the page, reads*)
"Three shots rang out. It only took a second, but in that lifetime Stone learned that three could, in fact, go into two." What was wrong with that? Why'd he change it?

DONNA:   He said he felt it telegraphed Alaura'd been shot, as well as Stone.

STINE:   If he wanted something else, for a better reason than just wanting something else, I could have given him something else. And a hell of a lot better than this. Why'd he have to do it while I was in New York?

DONNA (*Pointedly*): It was a big weekend for everyone, wasn't it?

STINE (*Ignoring that*): What was the rush to have this scene? It's the last one in the picture.

DONNA: He's going to shoot it first. It helps the budget.

STINE: He can't shoot this! It's full of holes. Christ, he's got Mallory in it! I've written an earlier scene where she's killed. I've got Mallory dead, he bounces her back to life — and vice versa, I'm sure. Does he realize how many changes these changes require? Is it possible someone can write, without knowing how to read?
(*Reading from the script*)
"Wild, bloodshot private eyes?" That's atrocious! Am I supposed to run up and down the aisles in every movie house in the country and say I didn't write that?

DONNA: I thought it was clever, to be honest.

STINE (*Realizing*): It's yours. It's your line.

DONNA: I tried to make it sound like you.

STINE: It doesn't rub off. Sometimes not even on me.

DONNA: I was covering for you. He'd have made it a lot worse, if I hadn't helped.

STINE: "Helped?" You'd need a divining rod to find the word "grateful" in me. Jesus, where the hell is everybody when they first deliver the typing paper? Where are all the "helpers" when those boxes full of silence come in? Blank. Both sides. No clue, no instructions enclosed on how to take just twenty-six letters and endlessly rearrange them so that you can turn them into a mirror of a part of our lives. Try it sometime. Try doing what I do before *I* do it.

DONNA:   You don't mind including *her* in your work.

STINE:   Her involvement's aimed at getting *me* to be the best possible me. She doesn't want to be me herself. What's left? Any other surprises? Any more little changes? Stone going to be played by Betty Hutton?

DONNA:   I'll tell him you want to see him.

STINE:   But in your own words. I'm sure they'll sound just like me. Maybe better.
(DONNA *turns to go, stops at:*)
Donna. I thought we meant something to each other.

DONNA (*Before exiting*):   Funny. I never got that impression.

STINE (*Sings*):
Funny, how'd I fail to see this little bedtime tale was
Funny?
I could cry to think of all the irony I missed,
What an unusual twist
Right at the end of it.

Funny,
Who could see that this pathetic scene would be
So funny?
Once you strain to find the grain of humor
Underneath,
Life double crosses with style,
Forcing you into a smile
So it can kick you in the teeth.

Just desserts,

We can laugh till it hurts.
At my expense
I'm accustomed to working on spec.
I always pick up the check.

I think it's funny.
Who could top or make this comic op'ra more
Compelling?
You could weave in some deceit to even up the score.
You'd have us all on the floor.
That would be roaringly funny.
Sad enough, my life's a joke that suffers in the telling,
Just another hoary chestnut from the bottom drawer,
I've heard so often before
That I can't laugh anymore.
(He turns upstage, and enters:)

*Scene 19*

*A studio sound stage. Hammering, sawing, ring-*
*ing. The storm before the calm. The set is the*
KINGSLEY *solarium.* DONNA *types at a small table.*
AVRIL *has make-up applied.* GERALD PIERCE, *who*
*plays* PETER, *runs his lines.* WERNER KRIEGER,
*who plays* LUTHER, *wears a robe, smokes a pipe.*
BUDDY, *beside* CARLA's *costumed* STAND-IN,
*watches the* CINEMATOGRAPHER *in the solarium*
*set.*

BUDDY (*Looking up*):   Okay, Bill, that's good!
           (*To* CINEMATOGRAPHER)
   Is that good for you, Jack?

CINEMATOGRAPHER:   Okay, that's good.
           (*Looking up*)
   Very good, Bill. Okay for you, Buddy?

BUDDY:   Perfect.
           (*Looking up*)
   Just put a silk in that, Bill, and bring it down.

CINEMATOGRAPHER (*Looking up*):   Bring it down, Bill.

BUDDY (*Looking up*):   Much better. More! More! Move it!
           (*The* STAND-IN *moves. He stops her*)
   Not you, darling.

STAND-IN:   Sorry, Mr. Fidler.

BUDDY:   Don't be nervous, sweetheart. It's only a movie.
>    (*Returning her to her position, he pats her behind,
>    comfortingly, yells to a crew member who is wheel-
>    ing on the iron lung*)
>
>    Careful! Careful! This thing's got to be spotless.
>    (*Wiping it with his handkerchief*)
>    The audience should want to drive it home.
>    (*Enter* STINE, *script in hand*)

STINE (*Angrily, to* BUDDY):   You got a minute?

BUDDY:   For you? A minute twenty. Marked down from an
hour ninety-eight. Just give me a second.
>    (*Re iron lung*)
>    Put it in the set!
>    (*As the iron lung is wheeled into the set, to the*
>    CINEMATOGRAPHER)
>    It's looking much better, Jack!
>    (*Looking up*)
>    Get an inkie over there, Bill!

STINE (*To* BUDDY, *re script*):   What is this shit?

BUDDY:   Donna, don't just sit there helping. Do something.
>    (DONNA *exits. To* STINE)
>    We haven't even started shooting and already you're re-
>    viewing it?

STINE (*Showing the cover page*):   Screenplay by the *two* of us?

BUDDY:   Take it easy.

STINE:   *We* wrote this? With *your* name on top?

BUDDY:   It's studio policy. They automatically put my name

on everything. We'll fix it.

STINE:   Why don't I believe you?

BUDDY:   Why? Because you're honest. Because you know in your heart-of-hearts that I was with you page-for-page; you *know* my name belongs there. On top, underneath, wherever.
> (*An arm around him*)

Stine, Stine, let's not spoil the first day. It's a wonderful script. Who cares who wrote what? Together, we made a beautiful child. We'll let the lawyers work everything out.
> (*To* PROP MAN)

What is that, Luther's soup? Let me check it!
> (*As he dips his finger into the bowl,* AVRIL *appears at his side*)

AVRIL (*Cozily*):   Good morning *again*, Mr. Fidler.

BUDDY (*Re soup*):   Needs salt.

PROP MAN:   Yes, sir.
> (*The* PROP MAN *exits*)

BUDDY (*Aside, to* AVRIL):   Six o'clock. My sauna.
> (*As he moves on,* AVRIL *crosses to* STINE)

AVRIL:   Hi.
> (*Reminding him*)

Avril.

STINE (*Unenthusiastically*):   French for April.

AVRIL:   I can't thank you enough for keeping Mallory alive. We both prayed so hard you would.

STINE:   Merde.

AVRIL:   What?

STINE (*With a tight smile*): Look it up.

BUDDY (*Re iron lung*): Werner! Come here, try this out!

WERNER: Looks awfully small and tight.

BUDDY: Said the sailor to the girl!
(*Calls to* GENE, *his Assistant Director*)
Gene! Can we start, while I'm still in the business? I could've shot a double feature by now!

GENE: Two minutes, sir!

NEPHEW (*Entering*): Uncle Buddy?

BUDDY (*Rejecting a cup of coffee, handed him by* NEPHEW): Too black!
(NEPHEW *exits, as* DONNA *brings on* CARLA, *costumed as* ALAURA)
Come here, beauty.

CARLA: Don't touch my turban.

BUDDY (*Doing just that*): Stine, is this her? Is this Alaura Kingsley down to the ground?

STINE (*To* CARLA, *sincerely*): You're perfection. For a start.

CARLA (*To* BUDDY): Don't you wish you'd said that?

STINE: It's only a matter of time.

BUDDY (*Finished with her turban*): Don't let anybody touch that.
(*Calls out*)
I'm short one star, somebody!
(*Taking* CARLA's *hand*)
Carlita?
(*To* STAND-IN, *dismissing her*)

186

Thanks, sweetheart.

CARLA (*Re iron lung*):   That thing gives me the chills.

BUDDY:   It's an actor's dream. This bum's going to get paid for looking at himself in a mirror all day.
(*To* WERNER)
Hop in, lover. It's post time.
(WERNER *removes his robe, to reveal he's in tennis shirt and shorts*)

WERNER:   I hate this.

BUDDY:   I'll slip in somebody nice at lunch. Wait! Hold it! Tuck your shirt in!

WERNER:   For God's sake, Buddy. Nobody'll know when I'm in there.

BUDDY:   *I'll* know. *I* have to believe who's in there, when you're in there. A Luther Kingsley would never play tennis with his shirt hanging out, no matter how paralyzed he was.
(NEPHEW *runs on, hands* BUDDY *his coffee cup*)

NEPHEW:   Better?

BUDDY:   Too white!
(*As* NEPHEW *exits,* PANCHO VARGAS *enters*)
Pancho!

PANCHO:   Amigo!

BUDDY:   You don't work today, do you? Donna, does Pancho —?

PANCHO:   Just came down to give you a good luck hickey!
(*He gives* BUDDY *a hug and kiss*)

BUDDY:   The man's beautiful — even when he doesn't have to be.

PANCHO (*Warmly, to* AVRIL):   Good luck, kid.
        (AVRIL *smiles nervously. Sotto, to* AVRIL)
When do I get to see you?

AVRIL:   Six fifteen.

BUDDY:   Okay! Can we, for God's sakes, go? Gene?! Donna?! Will someone please tell me why I'm missing a private eye?
        (*Offstage, someone is heard singing "Ya Gotta Look Out for Yourself." A beat, then* JIMMY POWERS *enters, singing, and dressed as* STONE, *trenchcoat, fedora, the works*)
Jimbo!
        (*Suddenly, to* STINE'*s further surprise,* STONE *appears at* STINE'*s side*)

STONE (*To* STINE, *incredulously*):   Jimmy Powers?
        (*Note: No one but* STINE *hears and sees* STONE)

JIMMY (*To* BUDDY):   What do you think?

BUDDY:   Perfection! And that's just for starters.

JIMMY:   I'm shaking like a leaf.

BUDDY:   You're going to be terrific. Even better, you're going to be good. Settle down.
        (NEPHEW *runs on and hands* BUDDY *his coffee*)

NEPHEW:   Okay?

BUDDY:   Just right!
                (*Handing it to* JIMMY)
    Here.

(As BUDDY *fiddles obsessively with* JIMMY's *trench-coat belt:*)

STONE (*To* STINE): What is this, a joke? Who's ever going to take me — *or* you — seriously again? A *crooner*? Playing me? A tenor I wouldn't give you two fives for? Guess they couldn't get Betty Hutton, right?

GENE: Ready when you are, Mr. Fidler.

BUDDY: Okay! Let's make a movie!

GENE: Let's make a movie!
(BUDDY *joins* GENE *and the* CINEMATOGRAPHER *on the camera crane platform. As the crane rises and all take their places:*)

STONE (*Fumes, to* STINE, *re* JIMMY): "He's never out of the Hit Parade." "His records don't sit in the stores a minute." *That's* why Buddy doesn't care what Powers is doing to his wife. *Arranged* for him to do what he's doing to her. Any more than *she* cares about what he's doing to Avril, which, of course, is what you were doing to Donna, till she turned around and did it to you.

GENE: Quiet on the set, please!

BUDDY: Let's try one, shall we?! Give me tempo! Give me energy. Gene?

GENE: Roll 'em!

SOUNDMAN: Speed!

CLAPPERBOY (*Using sticks*): "City of Angels," Scene 93, Take 1.

BUDDY: Now, please be wonderful, everybody. Aaand — action!

(CARLA, *as* ALAURA, *begins to spoon-feed* WERNER)

ALAURA: Slowly, darling. Measured breaths. Measured breaths. Let me wipe that tear. We all miss poor Dr. Mandril, don't we?
(*Thunder and lightning effects, as* JIMMY, *as* STONE, *appears*)
Good evening, Mr. Stone. My husband's just having his dinner.

JIMMY: The condemned man slurped a hearty meal?

STONE (*To* STINE, *in disgust*): Ever have anybody puke inside your head?

JIMMY (*To* ALAURA): It'd make a lovely picture. Considering his chances with you around, you'd have to use very fast film.

ALAURA (*To* LUTHER): Mr. Stone is a rather desperate man, darling. All sorts of people are after him; he's even wanted for murder.

JIMMY: Which explains the look in these wild, bloodshot private eyes.

STINE (*Loudly*): Cut!!
(*The word is a thunderbolt*)

BUDDY: Who said that?!
(*All eyes go to* STINE. *As the camera crane is lowered and* BUDDY *steps down; to* STINE)
Are you crazy? Nobody says "Cut" on a sound stage but me! If this building's on fire and everyone inside's drowning, nobody yells "Cut" but the director. It's the eleventh God damn commandment! It's an unwritten law — in letters twenty feet high!

STINE (*Quietly, provocatively*):   Cut.

BUDDY:   What're you, looking to get thrown off the set? Is that what you want? Is this some kind of New York, snot-nose revenge?
>    (STINE *crosses to* BUDDY *and hands him an object from his jacket pocket*)

BUDDY:   What's this?

STINE:   My pencil. Now, you don't have to envy it anymore.

STONE (*To* STINE):   I like that. Remember it.

BUDDY:   Gene!

GENE (*Anticipating*):   The cops?

BUDDY:   Get the cops!

GENE (*To the* NEPHEW):   Get the cops!

NEPHEW (*Starts to run off; stops*):   Real cops or ours?
>    (BUDDY's *glare sends* GENE *and the* NEPHEW *running off*)

BUDDY (*To* STINE):   I want you out of here! Out of this studio, out of this town, out of this business!

STINE:   I accept!
>    (*To everyone*)
You're all witnesses! We've got an ironclad, unbreakable, never-again, no-more-picture deal!
>    (*He tosses the script to* BUDDY)
It's all yours. In every sense. I've got a date with a box full of beautiful blank paper. It's time I got back to the reality of fiction.
>    (NEPHEW *rushes on with two* STUDIO COPS — *the*

*same actors who played* BIG SIX *and* SONNY)

BUDDY (*Re* STINE):   Him!
(*He strikes his fist into the palm of his other hand.*
GENE *and the* NEPHEW *repeat the gesture. The*
COPS *start beating up* STINE)

STONE (*To* STINE):   Belt 'em!

STINE:   Me??

STONE:   They're not tough.
(*Sitting at the typewriter*)
Except in your mind. Start using it!
(*So saying, he begins typing.* STINE, *thus activat-
ed, dispatches the* COPS *using his fists, feet, the
clapperboard and make-up powder puffs, relieving
one of the* COPS *of his gun in the process. When*
STINE *turns to the crowd, holding the gun in innocent triumph, throwing them all into a panic:*)

BUDDY (*Starting to leave*):   Somebody get this crazy maniac
out of here!
(STINE *raises his hands, freezing* BUDDY. STONE
*strikes the typewriter's X key several times.*
BUDDY *walks and talks himself backwards to his
starting point.* STINE *takes the screenplay from*
BUDDY *and throws it into the air. As the pages
flutter down, the entire company moves toward
him, muttering angrily*)

GENE:   Hey, get offa Buddy's set, Buster!

HAIRDRESSER:   The very idea!
(STINE *raises his arms, freezing the company.*
STONE *X's the typewriter. All move and speak*

*backwards to their previous positions and freeze
once more. Then:*)

STINE (*To* STONE):   You did it!

STONE:   *You* did!

STINE & STONE:   *We* did!
                              (*Sing*)
I'm nothing without you,
Without you I lack what it takes.
Unless we're combined
I have half a mind
To blow all my chances and breaks.
        (STINE *hands* STONE *the gun;* STONE *hands* STINE
        *a pencil*)
Without you I'm bupkis.
A flop who keeps dropping the ball.
It's time to stop quaking
Start taking the lead
And you are the singular buddy I need.

I'm nothing without you,
Without you I'm nothing . . .
        (STONE *gestures "Wait!," crosses to the desk, sits
        at the typewriter*)

STONE (*Spoken, to* STINE):   A Hollywood ending!
        (*He strikes a few keys on the typewriter and the
        giant doors at the back of the sound stage open to
        admit* GABBY, *who joins them, to the delight of the
        company, now unfrozen*)

STINE, STONE & GABBY (*Sing*):
I'm nothing without you.

193

STONE:
    No hero,

STINE:
    A zero,

STINE & STONE:
    That's me.

STINE, STONE & GABBY:
    With you by my side
    There's no better guide
    On how to be all I can be.
    I'm nowhere without you.
    To doubt you is where I went wrong.
    The script calls for fusing and using our smarts,
        (*As* STINE, STONE *and* GABBY *get on the crane platform*)
    And greatness can come of the sum of our parts.
            (*The entire company joins in*)

ALL:
    From now on I'm with you,
    And with you is where I belong.
        (*They finish singing joyously, looking up, as* STINE, STONE *and* GABBY, *atop the camera crane, are raised high above the stage. Curtain*)

# COSTUME DESIGNS
## BY
### *Florence Klotz*

*Stine*

*Stone*

195

Gabby

Bobbi

*Alaura*

*Carla*

197

*Pimp*

*Irwin S. Irving*

198

*Oolie*

*Donna*

199

*Margie's Girls*

*Avril Raines*

**Larry Gelbart** has written for radio, television, film and the stage. His radio credits include *Duffy's Tavern*, Jack Parr and Bob Hope, and for television, "The Bob Hope Show," "Caesar's Hour," "The Danny Kaye Show," for which he received a Peabody Award, and the Art Carney specials, for which he received a Sylvania Award. He developed and co-produced with Gene Reynolds the television series *M\*A\*S\*H*, which earned him an Emmy Award, Peabody Award, Humanitas Award and several Writers Guild of America Awards. His screenplays include *The Notorious Landlady* (1960), *The Wrong Box* (1966, co-authored with Burt Shevelove), *Oh, God!* (1977), for which he received the Writers Guild of America Award, Edgar Allen Poe Award and an Oscar nomination, *Movie, Movie* (1981), and *Tootsie* (1982), which received the Los Angeles and New York Film Critics Awards, National Film Critics Award and nominations for the Oscar and British Academy Award. For the stage he wrote the books for the musicals *The Conquering Hero* (1961), *A Funny Thing Happened on the Way to the Forum* (1962, in collaboration with Burt Shevelove) and *City of Angels* (1989), and his plays include *Jump* (1971), *Sly Fox* (1976, based on Ben Jonson's *Volpone*) and *Mastergate* (1989). He received Tony Awards for *A Funny Thing Happened on the Way to the Forum* and *City of Angels*, and a second Edgar Allen Poe Award for the latter, as well as a Drama Desk Award and a special award from the Outer Critics Circle for his contributions to comedy (*Mastergate* and *City of Angels*). Mr. Gelbart is a member of the Dramatists Guild, the Writers Guild of America West, the Writers Guild of Great Britain, ASCAP, and the Directors Guild.

**Cy Coleman** composed the music for the Broadway musicals *Wildcat* (1960), *Little Me* (1962), *Sweet Charity* (1966), *Seesaw* (1973), *I Love My Wife* (1977), *On the Twentieth Century* (1978), and *Barnum* (1980). He has scored such films as *Father Goose*, *Power*, *Garbo Talks*, *Sweet Charity* (for which he won an Oscar nomination) and *Family Business*, and for television he wrote the Shirley MacLaine specials "If They Could See Me Now" and "Gypsy in My Sole" (for which he won three Emmy Awards). Mr. Coleman has been honored with 12 Grammy nominations, seven Tony nominations (winning that award twice for *On the Twentieth Century* and *City of Angels*), Drama Desk Awards (for *On the Twentieth Century* and *City of Angels*) and the Irvin Feld Humanitarian Award from the National Conference of Christians and Jews. He is the president of Notable Music Company and serves on the Board of Directors of ASCAP.

**David Zippel** has contributed lyrics to the off-Broadway revues *A. . . My Name Is Alice* and *Diamonds*, and with composer Doug Katsaros he wrote the musical comedy *Just So*. A revue of his songs entitled *It's Better With a Band* played off Broadway and in London's West End. He wrote the original songs for *5, 6, 7, 8 . . . Dance!*, which starred Sandy Duncan at Radio City Music Hall, and his songs have been performed by such theater, cabaret and recording artists as Michael Feinstein, Gregory Hines, Lonette McKee, Debbie Shapiro and Ann Reinking. With Wally Harper he has written songs for the singer Barbara Cook, including "It's Better With a Band," and the original songs for her recent New York and West End concert, *Barbara Cook: A Concert for the Theater*. Mr. Zippel makes his Broadway musical comedy debut with *City of Angels* and received a Tony Award and Drama Desk Award for his lyrics.